Между нами

Домáшние задáния
Homework Assignments

Units 1-5

Last Revised: June 2, 2020 *

by
William J. Comer
Portland State University

with **Lynne deBenedette**
Brown University

and **Alla Smyslova**
Columbia University

Except as otherwise noted, this work is licensed under a
Creative Commons Attribution-NonCommercial-NoDerivatives 4.0 International License.

Между нами

Домáшние задáния (Homework Assignments): Units 1-5
Last Revised: June 2, 2020

(cc) 2015. This work was originally published by the Ermal Garinger Academic Resource Center at the University of Kansas. Editions subsequent to 2018 are published by the Open Language Resource Center (http://olrc.ku.edu/).

Illustrations: Anna Boyles
Production/Layout Coordinator: Keah Cunningham
Project Assistant: Kayla Grumbles
Project Manager: Jonathan Perkins

Printed by Jayhawk Ink
University of Kansas

Except as otherwise noted, this work is licensed under a Creative Commons Attribution-NonCommercial-NoDerivatives 4.0 International License.

You are free to copy and redistribute the material in any medium or format under the following terms:

- **Attribution** — You must give appropriate credit, provide a link to the license, and indicate if changes were made. You may do so in any reasonable manner, but not in any way that suggests the licensor endorses you or your use.
- **NonCommercial** — You may not use the material for commercial purposes.
- **NoDerivatives** — If you remix, transform, or build upon the material, you may not distribute the modified material.
- **No additional restrictions** — You may not apply legal terms or technological measures that legally restrict others from doing anything the license permits.

To view a full copy of this license, visit http://creativecommons.org/licenses/by-nc-nd/4.0/ or send a letter to Creative Commons, 444 Castro Street, Suite 900, Mountain View, California, 94041, USA.

ISBN: 978-1611950298

Содержа́ние

Введе́ние v

Уро́к 1 .... **1**
    Часть 1 1
    Часть 2 19
    Часть 3 33

Уро́к 2 .... **49**
    Часть 1 49
    Часть 2 63
    Часть 3 77

Уро́к 3 .... **93**
    Часть 1 93
    Часть 2 109
    Часть 3 125

Уро́к 4 .... **143**
    Часть 1 143
    Часть 2 159
    Часть 3 173

Уро́к 5 .... **185**
    Часть 1 185
    Часть 2 197
    Часть 3 211

Введе́ние

To Students

Welcome to the study of Russian! *Дома́шние зада́ния* (Homework Assignments) provides listening and written activities that you will complete at home and then turn in to your instructor. It is only one element of the *Ме́жду на́ми* program, which also includes an online textbook (mezhdunami.org) and *Рабо́та в аудито́рии* (Classroom Activities).

Organization of these homework exercises

The numbering system in the homework exercises matches the numbering system in the online textbook. As such, the exercises labeled 2.4 correspond to episode 2.4 Но́вые адреса́ in the online textbook.

Within each episode, exercises start with work on the episode's text, then move to particular vocabulary and grammar work, and conclude with more open-ended writing (often situations or paragraphs about yourself). The exercises at the start of a unit are intended as building blocks - words, phrases and constructions that you can use (and reuse) in the open-ended writing exercises, and in many other contexts. Maximizing your use of these building blocks will make later assignments much easier, and it will help you gauge how well you have acquired the new material in the unit.

Read the instructions for each exercise carefully and follow the steps as indicated. Pay careful attention as you work through the individual elements of each activity, as you are often asked to understand subtle differences in meaning.

🎧 marks listening activities where you will need to work with a recording located on the А́удио tab of the *Ме́жду на́ми* website.

🔍 marks activities where you will need to do information gathering on Russian internet sites.

Learning strategies to keep in mind as you do homework:
1. Regularly review the texts and grammar explanations in current and previous episodes of the online textbook. Language learning is cumulative, and each new homework exercise relies on previously learned material.
2. Work actively on sounding out new words you encounter in the exercises. You will be surprised at how many international words you will recognize once you pronounce syllables aloud. If you still do not recognize the word, check it in the online dictionary on the *Ме́жду на́ми* website. Since words can often have multiple meanings and usages, working with the *Ме́жду на́ми* dictionary will help you narrow down the set of word meanings to those that you have encountered.
3. When you are working on a specific exercise, try to complete as much of it as you can by drawing only on your memory of what you have learned from the textbook and your classroom practice. When you have finished this first attempt, check your work against the texts and grammar explanations and fill in any details you could not recall. This approach is more efficient in terms of time than looking up individual words or word forms as you encounter them. Furthermore, trying an exercise from memory first will give you a sense of how well you have internalized the material. If you can do an exercise easily AND correctly, then you should have confidence in your command of that material. If you try an exercise and cannot do it at all, you should go back and work with the text and grammar explanations before attempting it.

4. As you review your first attempt at doing a written exercise, pay attention to spelling. Have you confused **о** / **а**? Are there tails on the letters **ц** and **щ**? And a hook over **й**?
5. When doing the open-ended writing exercises, do not look up new and unknown words and phrases in online translators. Use the words and phrases that you have already seen in the texts and activities.

Unlike other language textbooks that you may have used, the activities in this homework packet require you to pay attention to the meanings of new words and phrases, and not just to their grammar. To complete many of these activities you will need to know the texts and the story line of *Ме́жду на́ми*.

Имя и фамилия: _____   Число: _____

Уро́к 1: часть 1

1.1 Упражне́ние А. Кто э́то?

Below are some American first names written in Russian letters. Sound out the names and then place a check mark in the appropriate column to indicate whether the name is more typical for a man or for a woman.

	он	она́
1. Стив	____	____
2. Росс	____	____
3. Ро́дни	____	____
4. Ка́рен	____	____
5. Э́рика	____	____
6. Викто́рия	____	____
7. Дэ́вид	____	____
8. Мэ́ри	____	____
9. Гре́та	____	____
10. Ло́ра	____	____
11. Сама́нта	____	____

Между нами: Дома́шние зада́ния

Имя и фамилия: _____ Число: _____

1.1 Упражнéние Б. Notice the Difference

Print	Cursive	Print	Cursive	Print	Cursive
А а	*А а*	К к	*К к*	Х х	*Х х*
Б б	*Б б*	Л л	*Л л*	Ц ц	*Ц ц*
В в	*В в*	М м	*М м*	Ч ч	*Ч ч*
Г г	*Г г*	Н н	*Н н*	Ш ш	*Ш ш*
Д д	*Д д*	О о	*О о*	Щ щ	*Щ щ*
Е е	*Е е*	П п	*П п*	ъ	*ъ*
Ё ё	*Ё ё*	Р р	*Р р*	ы	*ы*
Ж ж	*Ж ж*	С с	*С с*	ь	*ь*
З з	*З з*	Т т	*Т т*	Э э	*Э э*
И и	*И и*	У у	*У у*	Ю ю	*Ю ю*
Й й	*Й й*	Ф ф	*Ф ф*	Я я	*Я я*

Use the alphabet table above to help you notice important differences between cursive and printed letters. Then, read the following descriptions of cursive Russian letters. Choose the letter that best matches the description and place a check mark next to it. The first one has been done for you.

The Russian lower-case cursive letter …   Print letter
0. looks like an English cursive letter **m**.   ___ м   ✓ т

1. is "tall" and comes up to the top line.   ___ в   ___ к

2. has a circle on the lower left and a tail that rises and points to   ___ д   ___ б
   the right.

3. rises into a single curve on top, and comes down into a second   ___ г   ___ ч
   curve.

4. starts with a hook and has a single pointed peak.   ___ л   ___ п

Имя и фамилия: _____   Число: _____

5. looks like an English cursive letter **g**.   ___ д   ___ г
6. starts with a hook and has two pointed peaks.   ___ м   ___ т
7. rises into a broad flat horizontal line and then descends.   ___ г   ___ ч

1.1 Упражне́ние B. У́чимся чита́ть кири́ллицу (Learning to Read Cursive)

Match the cursive form of each word to its printed equivalent by writing the appropriate letter in the blank next to the cursive word. The first one has been done for you.

#	cursive		printed
0.	_и_ плуг	а.	так
1.	___ мак	б.	е́вро
2.	___ до́лго	в.	ла́па
3.	___ е́вро	г.	ли́га
4.	___ ли́га	д.	вал
5.	___ так	е.	до́лго
6.	___ дал	ж.	мак
7.	___ ла́па	з.	дал
8.	___ э́ра	~~и.~~	~~плуг~~
9.	___ вал	к.	гид́а
10.	___ гид́а	л.	э́ра

Между нами: Дома́шние зада́ния   Уро́к 1: часть 1   3

Имя и фамилия: _____ Число: _____

1.1 Упражне́ние Г. У́чимся писа́ть бу́квы (Learning to Write Letters)
Practice writing the cursive letter as many times as you can in the space provided.

К к *Ƙ ƙ*

М м *М м*

Т т *Т̄ т̄*

А а *А а*

О о *О о*

Notes on individual letters:

1. The cursive version of the letter **м** will always have an initial hook. This helps separate it from other letters, and makes it more obvious in a connected word.

2. The cursive **т** has some variation in how it can be written. The true cursive version is sometimes written with a bar over it, which helps separate it from other letters. Look at the word **а́том**:

а̄том

Some Russians write the the cursive letter as a version of a lower-case print **т** -- note, however, that it does not resemble an English small **t**.

так

3. The letter **о** ends on the top of the line. Many Russians will not connect it if the following letter starts at the bottom of the line, like the letters **м** or **л**; the word **а́том** below illustrates this. Others will connect the letter **о** to letters that start at the top like **к**, and loop around to connect it to letters that start at the bottom, as you can see in the word **ко́ка-ко́ла**.

атом   *кока-кола*

4 Уро́к 1: часть 1 *Между нами*: Дома́шние зада́ния

Имя и фамилия: _____   Число: _____

1.1 Упражнение Д. Учимся писать слова (Learning to Write Words)

Now practice writing words using these letters in cursive. The English equivalents are given in parentheses. Your instructor may ask you to write in the stress marks.

мама
(mama)

атом
(atom)

кот
(cat)

ком
(lump)

так
(thus, so)

мак
(poppy)

там
(there)

мат
(checkmate)

кто
(who)

A note about cursive and "joining" letters:
Not all letters have to be connected. Those of you who do not write in cursive in English may find it daunting at first to join the letters. Note that Russians themselves do not always connect the letters when they write. It may help to concentrate first on making sure your writing is in cursive (i.e., do not block print), and then work gradually toward joining letters when appropriate. A good strategy is to write the letters that make up a word close together, even if you are writing each letter separately. Pay attention to the models of Russian handwriting you see in these pages; we have shown you different examples of Russians' writing for precisely that reason. Most students' Russian cursive evolves as they progress and get more experience writing.

Между нами: Домашние задания   Урок 1: часть 1

Имя и фамилия: _____   Число: _____

1.1 Упражнéние Е. У́чимся писáть бу́квы
Practice writing the cursive letter as many times as you can in the space provided.

В в *В в*

Р р *Р р*

Н н *Н н*

С с *С с*

У у *У у*

Э э *Э э*

A note on individual letters:
The tail of the upper-case **У** does not dip below the line.

1.1 Упражнéние Ж. У́чимся писáть словá
Now practice writing words using these letters in cursive. The English equivalents are given in parentheses. Your instructor may ask you to write in the stress marks.

мáсса (mass) *масса*

трон (throne) *трон*

э́ра (era) *эра*

Марс (Mars) *Марс*

Имя и фамилия: _____   Число: _____

су́мма _*сумма*_
(sum)

Варва́ра _*Варвара*_
(Barbara)

1.1 УПРАЖНЕ́НИЕ 3. У́ЧИМСЯ ПИСА́ТЬ БУ́КВЫ

Practice writing the cursive letter as many times as you can in the space provided.

Г г   *Гг*

Д д   *Дд*

Л л   *Лл*

П п   *Пп*

Ш ш   *Шш*

Й й   *Йй*

Notes on individual letters:

1. The Russian letter **ш**, unlike the English letter "w", ends with the last stroke coming all the way down to the bottom. Compare the Russian word **шала́ш** (hut) and the English word "wallow":

   шалаш   *wallow*

2. The "hook" over **й** is <u>not</u> optional.

Имя и фамилия: _____ Число: _____

1.1 Упражнéние И. Учимся писáть бýквы

Practice writing the cursive letter as many times as you can in the space provided.

Я я   *Я я*

Е е   *Е е*

Ю ю   *Ю ю*

И и   *И и*

1.1 Упражнéние К. Place Cards

Practice your Russian cursive by writing out place cards for the first three characters from our story. In the fourth box, write your own first and last name in Russian cursive.

| Амáнда Ли | Антóнио Морáлес |
| Денис Гýрин | [Your Name] |

Имя и фамилия: _____   Число: _____

1.1 Упражнéние Л. Учимся писáть словá

Now practice writing words using these letters in cursive. The English equivalents are given in parentheses. Your instructor may ask you to write in the stress marks.

Ялта
(Yalta)

лáмпа
(lamp)

Мáша
(Masha)

май
(May)

Юрий
(Yuri)

иЮня
(of June)

áвгуст
(August)

дóлго
(a long time)

Урá!
(hurray!)

дрáма
(drama)

грамм
(gram)

Между нами: Домáшние задáния

Имя и фамилия: _____   Число: _____

Са́ша
(Sasha)

Notes on connecting letters in words:

1. Like **м**, the letters **л** and **я** also have a small initial hook to separate them from the previous letter. The initial hook on the letter **л** distinguishes it from the cursive version of the letter **г**. Notice in the words **Ма́льта** (Malta) and **ма́гма** (magma) how important the hooks are on the **л** and the **м** in the middle of the words.

2. When the letter **ш** immediately precedes or immediately follows the letter **и**, it can be hard to distinguish in some people's handwriting. A good example is the word **пиши́те** (write) or the name **Ми́ша**. Some Russians will draw a bar line under the "scoops" that are part of the **ш** to distinguish it from the other letters:

1.2 Упражне́ние А. У́чимся писа́ть бу́квы

Practice writing the cursive letter as many times as you can in the space provided.

Б б

З з

Ч ч

Ы

Ь

Notes on individual cursive letters:

1. The tail of the upper-case letter **З** does not dip below the line. When you write a capital **З** remember to make an inward curve in the middle; the letter **Э**, as in **Э́то**, does not have that curve. Compare the Russian spellings of these authors.

Эзо́п (Aesop)

Золя́ (Zola)

Имя и фамилия: _____ Число: _____

2. The relative size of your letters matters. A lower-case **в** should be as tall as your upper-case **В**, but **ы** and **ь** should be half the size of an upper-case letter. You can see these letters juxtaposed in the words **вновь** (anew) and **вы** (you):

   вновь *вы*

3. The lower-case **ч** has a broad flat top. This distinguishes it from the lower-case **г** whose upper portion is only a curve. Compare:

   час *газ*
   час (hour) газ (gas)

1.2 Упражнéние Б. У́чимся читáть кири́ллицу (Learning to Read Cursive)

Match the cursive form of each word to its printed equivalent by writing the appropriate letter in the blank next to the cursive word.

1. ____ *Áльпы*   а. нáчал
2. ____ *бáлами*   б. побьёт
3. ____ *начáл*   в. нагáн
4. ____ *повьём*   г. малы́ш
5. ____ *Я́лта*   д. шалáш
6. ____ *побьёт*   з. бáлами
7. ____ *вáлами*   к. Áльпы
8. ____ *нагáн*   л. вáлами
9. ____ *шалáш*   м. повьём
10. ____ *малы́ш*   н. Я́лта

Между нами: Домáшние задáния   Урóк 1: часть 1   11

Имя и фамилия: _____   Число: _____

1.2 Упражнéние B. Учимся писáть словá

Now practice writing words using these letters in cursive. The English equivalents are given in parentheses. Your instructor may ask you to write in the stress marks.

óбувь
(footwear)

зéбра
(an animal)

вы
(you)

Чарльз
(a male name)

Чебурáшка
(a cartoon character)

Читá
(a city)

мяч
(ball)

óчень
(very)

12   Урóк 1: часть 1   *Между нами*: Домáшние задáния

Имя и фамилия: _____   Число: _____

1.3 Упражне́ние А. У́чимся писа́ть бу́квы
Practice writing the cursive letter as many times as you can in the space provided.

Ф ф

Ж ж

Ё ё

Notes on individual letters:
1. If you are having trouble making **ж**, it might help to think of it in the following steps: first, a backwards "c," then an upstroke, a downstroke, and finish with a forwards "c."
2. Although Russians rarely write in the dots above **ё**, you should get in the habit of writing them in, both so that you know how to pronounce the letter, and so that you learn the word's stress.

Ме́жду на́ми: Дома́шние зада́ния   Уро́к 1: часть 1   **13**

Имя и фамилия: _____ Число: _____

1.3 Упражнение Б. Учимся читать кириллицу

Match the cursive form of each word to its printed equivalent by writing the appropriate letter in the blank next to the cursive word.

1. ___ *жирный*   а. пьёт
2. ___ *фотограф*   б. журнал
3. ___ *телефон*   в. жирный
4. ___ *новый*   г. льёт
5. ___ *льёт*   д. телефон
6. ___ *флейта*   е. новый
7. ___ *фонетика*   ж. флейта
8. ___ *журнал*   з. фотограф
9. ___ *пьёт*   и. лыжи
10. ___ *лыжи*   к. фонетика

1.3 Упражнение В. Учимся писать слова

Now practice writing words using these letters in cursive. The English equivalents are given in parentheses. Your instructor may ask you to write in the stress marks.

жира́ф *жираф* _____
(giraffe)

ёжик *ёжик* _____
(hedgehog)

Имя и фамилия: _____   Число: _____

телефо́н
(telephone) *телефо́н* _____

пьёт
(s/he drinks) *пьёт* _____

1.3 Упражне́ние Г. From Phrases to Conversations

Each picture below is accompanied by a short dialogue. Look at the English expressions on the left and complete the Russian version by filling in the missing word(s) for each speaker. Write your answers in cursive, and include the stress marks if your instructor has asked you to do so.

Диало́г 1

Who is that?	_____ э́то?
He is an American.	_____ америка́нец.
What is his name?	Как _____ зову́т?
His name is Kevin Dean.	Его́ зову́т _____ _____.

Имя и фамилия: _____ Число: _____

Диалог 2

What is your name?	Как _____ зову́т?
My name is Slava.	_____ зову́т Сла́ва.
My name is Andrei.	_____ зову́т Андре́й.
Very nice to meet you.	О́чень _____.

Диалог 3

What is her name?	Как _____ зову́т?
Nina.	_____.
Is she an undergraduate?	Она́ _____?
No, she is a graduate student.	Нет, она́ _____.

Имя и фамилия: _____   Число: _____

1.3 Упражнéние Д. Ситуáции (Situations)

Your written work will usually culminate in an assignment like this one where you apply what you have learned in real-life situations.

> **Use good communication strategies!**
> Before you start exercises like this one, it is a good idea to review the texts in recent episodes of the story. Recall the language you have seen and heard, and think about which phrases you might use in the given situation. 'f you cannot come up with phrases easily, you probably need to review the episodes again.

For each item, write out in Russian cursive what you would say. When you are finished, you will have created your side of a conversation that you might have with a group of visiting students from Russia.

1. On the way to the initial evening reception you run into your Russian teacher. How would you greet her in Russian?
   _____

2. At the reception you are standing next to one of the students. How would you ask one of them what his name is?
   _____

3. How would you tell him what your name is and say that you are happy to meet him?
   _____

4. How would you ask him if he is an undergraduate or a graduate student?
   _____

5. In the formal part of the reception, one of visitors makes a short speech in Russian. How would you ask the person next to you who it is making the speech?
   _____

6. At the end of the reception, how would you say goodbye to all of the visiting students?
   _____

7. The next morning you recognize one of the students as you are going to class. How would you say hi to her?
   _____

Между нами: Домáшние задáния   Урóк 1: часть 1

Имя и фамилия: _____ Число: _____

1.3 Упражнéние E. Putting It All Together

Write a dialogue of your own in which a Russian student and an American student exchange a greeting, find out each other's names, say something about themselves and close the conversation. Your dialogue should be about eight lines long. Be creative in using the Russian that you know to express your meaning.

Write your dialogue out in Russian cursive.

_____ : _____

_____ : _____

_____ : _____

_____ : _____

_____ : _____

_____ : _____

_____ : _____

_____ : _____

Имя и фамилия: _____   Число: _____

Урок 1: часть 2

1.4 Упражнéние А. Учимся писáть бýквы
Practice writing the cursive letter as many times as you can in the space provided.

X x   *Х х* _____

Ц ц   *Ц ц* _____

Щ щ   *Щ щ* _____

ъ   *ъ* _____

1.4 Упражнéние Б. Учимся писáть словá
Now practice writing words using these letters in cursive. The English equivalents are given in parentheses. Your instructor may ask you to write in the stress marks.

хорошó   *хорошо* _____

плóхо   *плохо* _____

пти́ца
(bird)   *птица* _____

Мо́царт   *Моцарт* _____

плащ
(raincoat) *плащ* _____

Имя и фамилия: _____ Число: _____

щенóк
(puppy)   *щенок*

объéкт   *объект*

субъéкт *субъект*

1.4 Упражнéние Б. Notice the Differences
Select the print letter on the right that matches the cursive letter described on the left.

The cursive letter …	Print letter	
1. is always "short" and never comes up to the top line.	___ ь	___ в
2. has a capital version with a tail that extends below the bottom line.	___ У	___ Ц
3. has a capital version that does not extend below the line.	___ Щ	___ З
4. always starts with a hook.	___ м	___ п
5. is never written with an initial hook.	___ л	___ г
6. has a hook and is written starting on the bottom left.	___ э	___ я

1.4 Упражнéние Г. Ýчимся писáть словá
Practice writing these Russian words in cursive. Then match the word to the appropriate picture by writing the letter of that picture (in cursive) in the blank provided. The first match has been done for you. If there are words that you do not know, you can look them up at
<u>wordreference.com/enru/</u>.

Словá	Cursive	Which picture?
0. щётка		*г*
1. царь		___
2. цирк		___
3. борщ		___

Урóк 1: часть 2   Мéжду нáми: Домáшние задáния

Имя и фамилия: _____ Число: _____

Слова	Cursive	Which picture?
4. пи́цца		____
5. конце́рт		____
6. аттракцио́н		____
7. я́хта		____
8. Теха́с		____

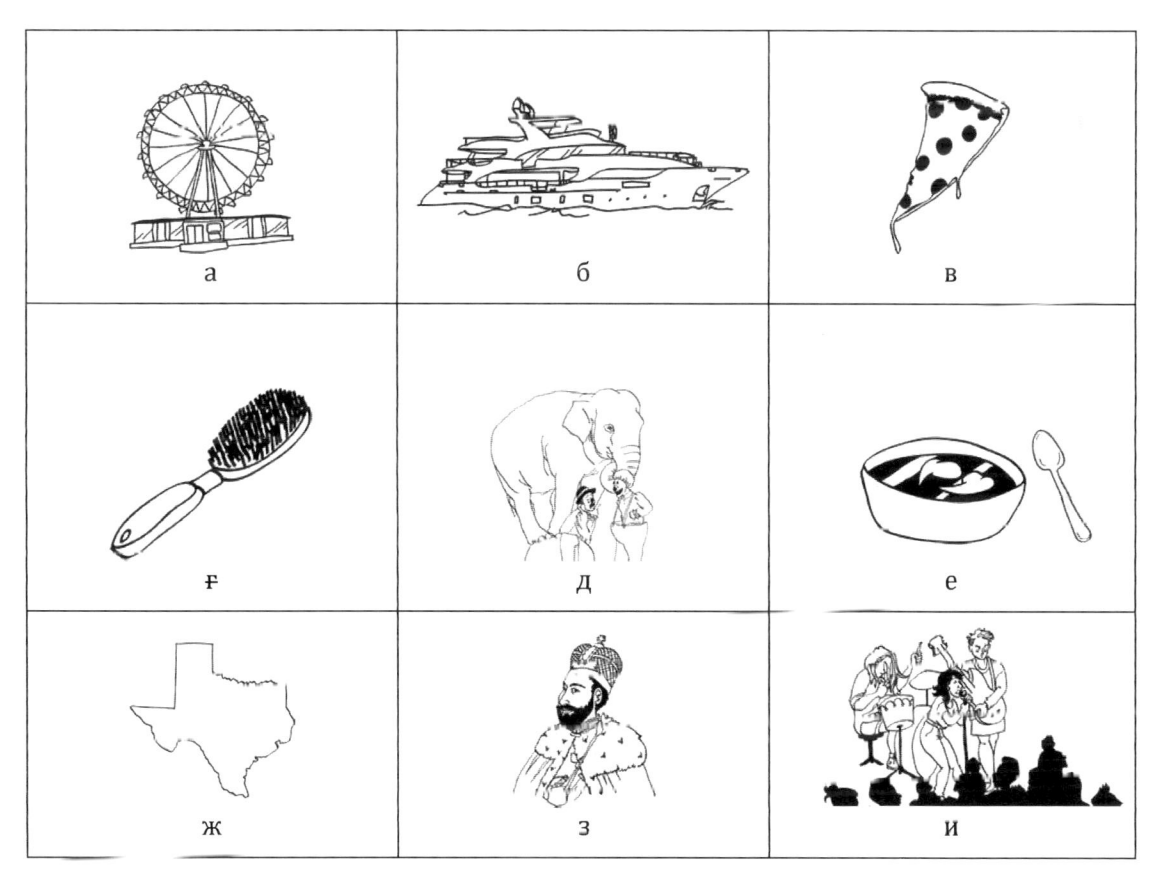

Между нами: Дома́шние зада́ния Уро́к 1: часть 2 21

Имя и фами́лия: _____ Число́: _____

1.4 Упражне́ние Д. Здра́вствуй и́ли здра́вствуйте?

Read through each situation and write the appropriate form of the greeting in the blank provided. Practice saying the word aloud as you write it. By the time you are finished, writing forms of this word should be much easier.

Здра́вствуй!	Здра́вствуйте!

1. Your Russian teacher walks into class that morning and says… _____

2. An old woman sees little Vanya, the grandchild of a neighbor, on the street and says… _____

3. Two adult neighbors who are acquaintances wind up together in the elevator of the apartment building and say… _____

4. You go to a regular meeting with your student conversation partner and greet her, saying… _____

5. You have started an internship and greet your boss every day, saying… _____

6. A child sees a neighbor, her parents' adult friend, and says… _____

7. Two colleagues who know each other only in the context of work but are not good friends say… _____

🎧 1.4 Упражне́ние Е. Paying Attention to Spelling

The dialogue below is between a study abroad director and her assistant. First listen to the recording and see if you can figure out what the conversation is about. Then listen again and write in the letters that are missing from the words in the dialog. If you need help, review the **текст** for this episode.

1. Summarize the dialogue in English.

   _____

2. Now fill in the blanks with the missing letters.

   – Как д__ла́?

   – Хор__шо́, с__аси́__ о.

   – На́__и аме__ика́н__ы уже́ зд__ь?

   – Да, __ от __ __й.

   – Отл´__ но.

Имя и фамилия: _____ Число: _____

1.4 Упражнение Ж. Наши герои

At this point you have been introduced to all four American students and two Russian representatives of the study abroad program. As you will follow these characters throughout future episodes, it is crucial that you recognize them. Write out their full names in cursive in the blanks below.

a. _____
б. _____
в. _____
г. _____
д. _____
е. _____

1.5 Упражнение А. Вопросы и ответы (Questions and answers)

Review episodes 1.4 and 1.5 and then match each question with its likely response. Note that there is one extra answer.

____ 1. Вы устали? a. Спасибо, хорошо.
____ 2. Где ваш багаж? б. Оно там.
____ 3. Где кафе? в. Немного.
____ 4. Как дела? г. Вот он.
____ 5. Где наши американцы? д. Она здесь.
  е. Вот они.

Между нами: Домашние задания   Урок 1: часть 2   23

Имя и фамилия: _____   Число: _____

1.5 Упражне́ние Б. Making Acquaintances

Here is a conversation between a teacher named Anna Ivanovna and two students, Vera and Tony. Use the word bank to fill in the words that are missing from their conversation. Write in cursive.

америка́нец	Извини́те	познако́мимся
про́сто	зову́т	О́чень
прия́тно	бага́ж	

А́нна Ива́новна: Здра́вствуйте! Дава́йте _____. Меня́ зову́т А́нна Ива́новна. Вас _____ Ве́ра, да?

Ве́ра: Да, меня́ зову́т Ве́ра. О́чень _____. А́нна Ива́новна, вот наш _____. Его́ зову́т Анто́нио Мора́лес.

А́нна Ива́новна: _____, что вы сказа́ли?

Ве́ра: Мора́лес. Анто́нио Мора́лес.

То́ни: Анто́нио, и́ли _____ То́ни. _____ прия́тно, А́нна Ива́новна.

1.5 Упражне́ние В. Ситуа́ции

You are at an airport on your first day in Russia. Write down what you would say in each of these situations. Review episodes 1.4 and 1.5 if you are having trouble recalling the phrases you need.

1. You greet the program administrator who is there to meet you.

   _____

2. You tell the administrator your name [*write your name in Russian*].

   _____

3. The administrator has said something, but you did not catch what she said.

   _____

4. You see a person pictured on a billboard ad and ask who it is.

   _____

5. You order tea in the café.

   _____

6. The server hands you your tea; thank her.

   _____

Имя и фамилия: _____   Число: _____

7. You want to know where the bathroom is.

   _____

8. You see the bathroom yourself.

   _____

1.5 Упражнéние Г. Меню́

Cafés often advertise a few menu items on small signs placed outside on the sidewalk; the menu items are often written in cursive. Identify the items on the sign below by writing the letter of the print version next to the corresponding item on the sign. Note that not all of the print menu items made it onto the sign.

Menu sign (cursive):
- чай
- пиво
- салаты
- капучино
- американо
- бутерброды
- айс-капучино

а. ко́фе
б. эспре́ссо
в. капучи́но
г. айс капучи́но
д. ла́тте
е. чай
ж. молоко́
з. минера́льная вода́
и. пи́во
к. сок
л. сала́ты
м. пи́цца
н. бутербро́ды
о. лимона́д
п. америка́но

What would you select to drink and eat if you were at this café at noon and had not yet had breakfast? Make your choices from the print menu and write them out in Russian cursive.

To drink: _____

To eat: _____

1.6 Упражнéние А. Vowels in Pairs

Complete the vowel chart by writing in the missing vowels in cursive.

Hard consonants are followed by …		э		о		
Soft consonants are followed by …	я		и			ю

Между нами: Домáшние задáния   Урóк 1: часть 2

Имя и фамилия: _____   Число: _____

1.6 Упражне́ние Б. Making Patronymics

When Russians think about baby names, they consider how the child's first name will sound together with the patronymic formed from the father's first name. Make first name and patronymic sets for the boy and girls below, using the father's first name from the left column. Boys' names are in the column labeled **ма́льчик**, and girls' names are in the column labeled **де́вочка**. The first one in each group has been done for you.

Гру́ппа 1. For boys, the patronymic is the father's name + **-ович**.
For girls, the patronymic is the father's name + **-овна.**

Father's name	ма́льчик	де́вочка
0. Анто́н	Вади́м Анто́нович	Светла́на Анто́новна
1. Степа́н	Алексе́й _____	Людми́ла _____
2. Ива́н	Серге́й _____	Еле́на _____
3. Макси́м	Евге́ний _____	О́льга _____
4. Влади́мир	Дми́трий _____	Раи́са _____
5. Алекса́ндр	Ю́рий _____	Ири́на _____
6. Марк	Гео́ргий _____	Татья́на _____
7. Михаи́л*	Илья́ Миха́йл_____	Со́фья Миха́йл_____

*Note: In the stem of this name, the **и** turns to **й** in the patronymic.

Гру́ппа 2. If the father's name ends in a soft consonant, the patronymic will be spelled **–евич** / **-евна.**

Make the patronymic for the opposite gender. Note the spelling of each name, and whether the letter before the patronymic ending is **–а**, **-е**, **-и** or **-ь**.

Father's name	ма́льчик	де́вочка
1. Серге́й	Вади́м _____	Светла́на Серге́евна
2. Никола́й	Евге́ний Никола́евич	О́льга _____
3. Гео́ргий	Серге́й _____	Еле́на Гео́ргиевна
4. Васи́лий	Ива́н Васи́льевич	Мари́я _____
5. Ю́рий	Алексе́й Ю́рьевич	Людми́ла _____

Имя и фамилия: _____ Число: _____

🎧 1.6 Упражнéние B. Reading Last Names in Cursive

You are in a Russian culture course, and your teacher has listed the last names of prominent Russians (e.g., writers, politicians, artists) in alphabetical order. Listen to the teacher talk about the order in which she will discuss these figures, and number the last names from one to twelve.

— *Горбачёв*　　　　　— *Толстой*

— *Достоевский*　　　— *Тургенев*

— *Плисецкая*　　　　— *Уланова*

— *Пугачёва*　　　　　— *Цветаева*

— *Пушкин*　　　　　— *Чехов*

— *Токарева*　　　　　— *Шагал*

Между нами: Домáшние задáния　　　　　Урóк 1: часть 2　　27

Имя и фамилия: _____   Число: _____

🔍 1.6 Упражнение Г. Известные имена-отчества (Famous Names and Patronymics)

This activity deals with **имя-отчество** combinations of famous Russians or characters from Russian literature. Most of these names are fairly common and could easily belong to anyone, but a few are unusual, and one is meant to be amusing. All of them are so strongly associated with a famous person that an internet search will show that person (or literary character) near the top of the search results.

1. Go to brief.ly/namesearch and use the links you find to search google.ru for the **имя-отчество** combinations listed below.
2. Use the information from your search to match each person to a description within the **Кто это?** box below. One has been done for you.
3. When you have matched the person, write in his/her **фамилия** in the space provided.

	имя-отчество	фамилия
2	Александр Сергеевич	Пушкин
___	Акакий Акакиевич	_____
___	Анна Андреевна	_____
___	Антон Павлович	_____
___	Владимир Владимирович	_____
___	Владимир Ильич	_____
___	Лев Николаевич	_____
___	Надежда Константиновна	_____
___	Настасья Филипповна	_____
___	Пётр Ильич	_____
___	Раиса Максимовна	_____
___	Софья Андреевна	_____

Кто это?

1. Heroine of the novel *The Idiot*
2. ~~Writer of prose and poetry, including *Boris Godunov*~~
3. Composer of *Swan Lake*
4. Author of *War and Peace*
5. Bolshevik and first Soviet leader
6. 20th century poet who lived in Leningrad
7. teacher and wife of the USSR's first and last president
8. Hero of Gogol's *The Overcoat*
9. Past and current Russian president
10. Wife of the author of *War and Peace*
11. Writer of plays, short-stories, but was trained as a physician
12. Revolutionary and wife of Владимир Ильич (above)

Имя и фамилия: _____ Число: _____

1.6 Упражнéние Д. When to Be Formal, and When to Be Informal

age 7, first grade	age 30, office worker	age 21, college student	age 14, ninth grade	age 63, teacher	age 59, chemist

1. Using the information provided above, imagine that you are the person depicted in the first illustration and that you are greeting the person in the second. Do you use the informal Здрáвствуй! or the formal Здрáвствуйте!? Assume that the people do not know each other.

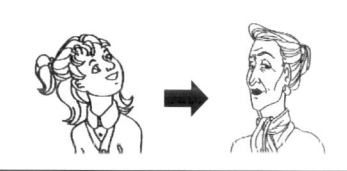

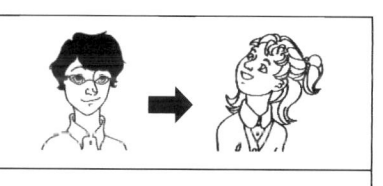

2. You have just found out that the teacher and the chemist are a married couple and that the teenager is their granddaughter. Imagine that you are the person depicted in the first illustration and that you are speaking to the person in the second. Do you use ты or вы?

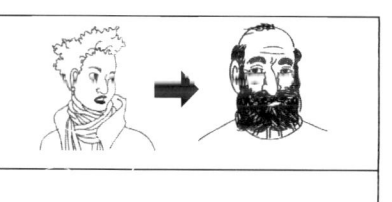

Между нами: Домáшние задáния   Урóк 1: часть 2   29

Имя и фамилия: _____ Число: _____

1.6 Упражнéние E. Personal Pronouns
Use the English cues to complete the questions and answers below.

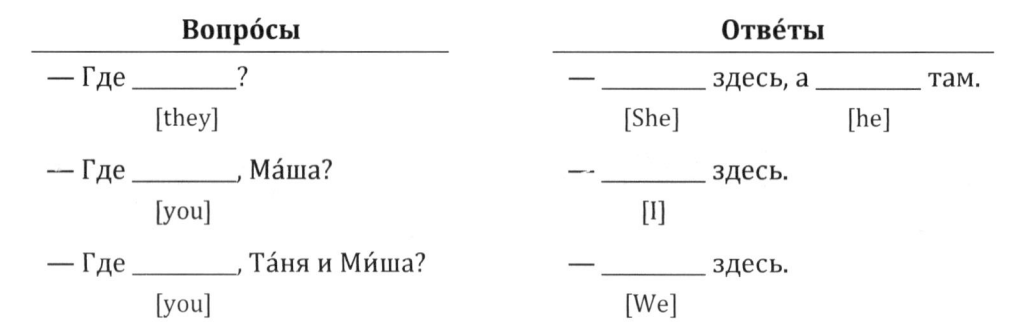

Вопрóсы	Отвéты
— Где _____? [they]	— _____ здесь, а _____ там. [She] [he]
— Где _____, Мáша? [you]	— _____ здесь. [I]
— Где _____, Тáня и Мúша? [you]	— _____ здесь. [We]

1.6 Упражнéние Ж. Ситуáции
Review the conversations that our characters have in Часть 2 and think about what you would say in the following situations. Write out the Russian phrases in cursive. Note that all of these prompts are related.

Your campus is hosting a group of visiting students and teachers from Russia for a few days.

1. As you are approaching your classroom, you see one of the teachers from the visiting group. How would you greet the teacher in Russian?
   _____

2. You actually wanted to catch the teacher to tell him/her about a student. How would you tell the teacher that it's great that s/he is already there?
   _____

3. How would you ask the teacher where Andrei is?
   _____

4. S/he has told you that s/he does not know where Andrei is. How would you respond to him/her that you understand.
   _____

Имя и фами́лия: _____   Число́: _____

1.6 Упражне́ние 3. Тепе́рь ваш диало́г!

Write a dialogue of your own in which you meet your Russian instructor for the first time. It is your choice whether your instructor is a man or a woman, but assume that s/he is about forty-five years old. Have the instructor initiate the conversation. Using appropriate etiquette, exchange a greeting and your names, and respond appropriately. Your dialogue should be at least four lines long. Be creative, but use the Russian that you know.

The name and patronymic of the instructor in my dialog is: _ _____

Write out your dialogue below, using the initials of the instructor and **я** to indicate who says what. Write in cursive.

_____ : _____

_____ : _____

_____ : _____

_____ : _____

_____ : _____

_____ : _____

_____ : _____

Между нами: Дома́шние зада́ния   Уро́к 1: часть 2   **31**

Имя и фамилия: _____ Числó: _____

Урóк 1: часть 3

1.7 Упражнéние A. Нóвые словá (New Words)
Use the words in the word bank to label the items in the picture below. Once you have finished, practice reading the words aloud and learning what they mean.

крéсло	кровáть	лáмпа
окнó	радиобудúльник	телевúзор
~~тýмбочка~~	телефóн	~~стол~~

1. _____
2. _____
3. _____
4. _____
5. тýмбочка _____
6. _____
7. _____
8. стол _____
9. _____

Между нами: Домáшние задáния

Имя и фамилия: _____ Число: _____

1.7 Упражне́ние Б. Кто э́то тако́й? Что э́то тако́е?

a. How would a curious Russian child ask about each of the pictures below? Place a check mark next to the appropriate question. Then, see if you can answer the question by writing out the name of the person or thing. Remember that **кто** is used for any animate being. The first one has been done for you.

✓ Кто э́то тако́й? ___ Что э́то тако́е? 0. Э́то <u>Чайко́вский</u>. [Он компози́тор.]	___ Кто э́то тако́й? ___ Что э́то тако́е? 1. Э́то _____.	___ Кто э́то тако́й? ___ Что э́то тако́е? 2. Э́то _____.
___ Кто э́то тако́й? ___ Что э́то тако́е? 3. Э́то _____.	___ Кто э́то тако́й? ___ Что э́то тако́е? 4. Э́то _____.	___ Кто э́то тако́й? ___ Что э́то тако́е? 5. Э́то _____.

б. Did you get them right? Check the answer key below and correct your answers if necessary.

[upside down:] 2. Э́то йо́гурт; 3. Э́то тигр, сиби́рский тигр; 4. Э́то самова́р; 5. Э́то гиппопота́м; 6. Э́то соба́ка.

Имя и фамилия: _____ Число: _____

1.7 Упражне́ние В. Но́вые слова́

Review the episode and note things Amanda and Caitlin have at the hotel. Make a list of at least six of those things that you also have here at school. Write in cursive.

_____   _____   _____

_____   _____   _____

_____

1.7 Упражне́ние Г. Noun Stems

Look carefully at the endings of the nouns in the left-hand column and place a check mark in the appropriate column on the right to indicate whether they end in a hard or soft stem.

		Hard Stem	Soft Stem
1.	пиани́ст	____	____
2.	о́тчество	____	____
3.	фами́лия	____	____
4.	сло́во	____	____
5.	слова́рь	____	____
6.	чай	____	____
7.	бу́ква	____	____
8.	администра́тор	____	____
9.	дя́дя	____	____
10.	крова́ть	____	____

Имя и фамилия: _____ Число: _____

1.8 Упражнéние А. Одéжда

Review the pictures of clothing in this episode, paying careful attention to how they are pronounced. Sort them into the following categories, saying each word aloud as you write it in the appropriate box. Try to find at least four items for each category. Write in cursive.

зи́мняя одéжда (winter)	лéтняя одéжда (summer)
óбувь (footwear)	аксессуáры [Sound out this word.]

🎧 1.8 Упражнéние Б. Одéжда

You will hear a description of what each person is wearing. Listen for the items of clothing and circle the items that you hear.

1.
2.
3.
4.

36 Урóк 1: часть 3   *Мéжду нáми*: Домáшние задáния

Имя и фамилия: _____ Число: _____

1.8 Упражне́ние В. Он, она́, оно́ или они́?

a. Lena and Dima are sharing a hotel room, but the room is so messy that Lena cannot find anything. Dima can easily point to all of the objects Lena is asking about. Complete Dima's responses to her questions with the Russian equivalent of "There it is." / "There they are." Remember that in Russian "it" can be expressed with the pronouns **он**, **она́**, **оно́**, or **они́**. Your choice of the pronoun will depends on the gender and number of the object. The first one has been done for you.

Ле́на:	Ди́ма:
0. Где твои́ джи́нсы?	Вот <u>они́</u>.
1. Где твой чемода́н?	Вот _____.
2. Где твоя́ футбо́лка?	Вот _____.
3. Где моё пла́тье?	Вот _____.
4. Где моя́ ю́бка?	Вот _____.
5. Где твоё пальто́?	Вот _____.
6. Где мои́ сапоги́?	Вот _____.
7. Где мой телефо́н?	Вот _____.
8. Где мой слова́рь?	Вот _____.

a. Now review the items that Lena and Dima were talking about. Circle the number of the sentence if you would definitely take that item with you on a beach vacation.

1.8 Упражне́ние Г. 7-Letter Spelling Rule

Complete the spelling rule by filling in the missing letters.

After ____, к, ____, ж, ____, ч, ____, always write ____, never ____.

Между нами: Дома́шние зада́ния   Уро́к 1: часть 3

Имя и фами́лия: _____ Число́: _____

1.8 Упражне́ние Д. Making Words Plural

Write out the plurals of the following nouns in cursive. Then circle any words whose endings reflect a 7-letter spelling rule change. Finally, label the words by theme: **О** = **оде́жда** (clothing); **Л** = **лю́ди** (people); **Ч** = **чте́ние** (reading material).

Singular	Plural	Theme
руба́шка	_____	____
аспира́нтка	_____	____
тетра́дь	_____	____
шарф	_____	____
журна́л	_____	____
газе́та	_____	____
студе́нт	_____	____
ту́фля	_____	____
ю́бка	_____	____
уче́бник	_____	____
ма́йка	_____	____
слова́рь	_____	____
журнали́ст	_____	____

1.8 Упражне́ние Е. Packing List

You are going away to a friend's house for a long winter weekend. Most of the time you will be dressing casually, but you may go out one night. Below is a packing list of possible clothing items, although the endings of the words are blank. Decide whether you would take one of these items or more than one, and write in the appropriate ending to make the item(s) singular or plural. If the noun does not have an ending in the singular, write in **Ø**. If you would not take the item at all, put a singular ending on the clothing item, and then put a line through the whole word.

1. костю́м____
2. джи́нс____
3. футбо́лк____
4. пиджа́к____
5. ма́йк____
6. ю́бк____
7. сви́тер____
8. плащ____
9. брю́к____
10. руба́шк____
11. ку́ртк____
12. ша́пк____

Имя и фамилия: _____ Число: _____

1.9 Упражнéние А. Рюкзáк

All of these items can typically be found in a student's backpack. Label the items below in cursive, using the word bank to identify them.

ноутбу́к	тетрáдь	дéньги
телефóн	учéбник	газéта
рýчка	ключ	карандáш

1.  _____ 2.  _____ 3. _____

4.  _____ 5.  _____ 6. _____

7.  _____ 8.  _____ 9. _____

🎧 1.9 Упражнéние Б. Это мой рюкзáк.

At the airport, someone picked up Tony's backpack by mistake. In order to prove it is his, Tony tells the person what is in it. Listen to what he says and put a check mark by each item in 1.9 Упражнéние А that he mentions.

Между нами: Домáшние задáния Урóк 1: часть 3 39

Имя и фамилия: _____   Число: _____

1.9 Упражнéние B. Ownership

a. Label these pictures in Russian. Write in cursive.

1.  _____   2.  _____   3. _____

4.  _____   5.  _____   6. _____

7.  _____   8.  _____   9. _____

10.  _____   11.  _____   12. _____

б. Pick six of the objects above and "claim them" by putting a check mark next to them. Then write six full sentences, one about each object, saying, "This is my _____." Your sentences should be in Russian and in cursive.

1. _____
2. _____
3. _____
4. _____
5. _____
6. _____

40   Урóк 1: часть 3   *Мéжду нами*: Домáшние задáния

Имя и фамилия: _____ Число: _____

в. You do not know to whom the rest of the objects belong. Ask your roommate whose they are, using the appropriate possessive pronoun (**чей**, **чья**, **чьё**, or **чьи**) in each of your questions.

0. Чьи это кроссо́вки? (*Whose sneakers are these?*) _____
1. _____
2. _____
3. _____
4. _____
5. _____
6. _____

1.9 Упражне́ние Г. Asking About Ownership

Using the context provided, fill in the missing possessives to complete the conversations below. Remember, that the possessive of the informal **ты** is **твой** and that the possessive of the formal or plural **вы** is **ваш**.

1. *Конте́кст:* Natalya Mikhailovna is speaking with Amanda and Caitlin.

   Ната́лья Миха́йловна: Де́вушки, э́то _____ тетра́ди?

   Ама́нда: Вот э́то _____ тетра́дь. А я не зна́ю, _____ э́то тетра́дь. Ке́йти, она́ _____?

   Ке́йтлин: Нет, не _____.

2. *Конте́кст:* Tony and Josh are standing on the street outside the hotel. Denis is pointing up at the building.

   Дени́с: То́ни, Джош, э́то _____ окно́?

   Джош: Да, э́то _____ окно́.

3. *Конте́кст:* Natalya Mikhailovna and Denis have got the students' passports back from the hotel administrator and are sorting through them.

   Дени́с: Ната́лья Миха́йловна, _____ э́то докуме́нты? Э́то па́спорт То́ни, да?

   Ната́лья Миха́йловна: Да, э́то _____ па́спорт. А Ке́йтлин и Ама́нда — где _____ докуме́нты?

   Дени́с: Вот они́.

Имя и фами́лия: _____ Числó: _____

1.10 Упражне́ние А. Numbers
The following phone numbers are written out as words. Write them out as numbers.

1. де́вять-оди́н-три шесть-пять-три три-де́вять-четы́ре-ноль: _____
2. четы́ре-ноль-оди́н семь-во́семь-два во́семь-де́вять-три-два: _____
3. шесть-два-семь де́вять-оди́н-пять де́сять-оди́н-пять: _____

1.10 Упражне́ние Б. Ваш телефо́н
Write out your phone number (as words) in Russian. Follow the example set in the previous exercise. Practice reading your number aloud until you are comfortable saying it in Russian.

_____ _____ _____ -

_____ _____ _____ -

_____ _____ _____ _____

1.10 Упражне́ние В. Addresses
Your friend who knows no Russian needs to find the addresses below. She can recognize the names of the streets. Write the numbers as digits above the Russian words so that she can find the residence.

1. Ле́нинский проспе́кт, дом семь, ко́рпус четы́ре, кварти́ра во́семь

2. Тверска́я у́лица, дом пять, ко́рпус два, кварти́ра де́сять

1.10 Упражне́ние Г. Translations
Translate these small dialogues into Russian. Be sure to write the names of the speakers in Russian as well. Write your sentences in cursive.

1. Oleg: Whose backpack is that?

   Galya: It's my backpack.

   _____

   _____

2. Oleg: Is this your address?

   Lena and Masha: No. It's not our address.

   _____

   _____

3. Tanya: What's your phone number?

   Masha: My phone number is 123-45-67.

   _____

   _____

Имя и фамилия: _____ Число: _____

4. Ira: Where are their books?

   Andrei: They are (over) there.

   _____
   _____

5. Nina: Whose money is that?

   Anton: I don't know.

   _____
   _____

1.10 Упражнéние Д. Ситуáции

Review all of the episodes in Часть 3 and write out what you would say in Russian if you were in the following situations. Note that all of these prompts are connected.

1. You want to talk to your new Russian teacher Anna Ivanovna during her office hours in the early afternoon. You knock on the door. How do you ask if you may come in?

   _____

2. You walk in. How do you greet your teacher?

   _____

3. Your group is rather large, and you are not sure your teacher has remembered everyone's name. How do you remind your teacher of your name?

   _____

4. How would your teacher ask you if everything is okay?

   _____

5. Towards the end of your conversation with your teacher you notice an unusual stuffed animal on a shelf. Ask your teacher about it. [*Remember that animals are animate!*]

   _____

6. Your teacher picks up the stuffed animal and tells you that it is *Cheburashku*.

   _____

7. Your teacher printed you a picture of *Cheburashku*. As you leave, say thank you and goodbye.

   _____

Между нами: Домáшние задáния   Урóк 1: часть 3   43

Имя и фамилия: _____   Число: _____

🔍 1.10 Упражнéние Е. Фáкты. Собы́тия. Лю́ди. (Facts. Events. People.)

a. Fill in the blanks below with information about the status of Russian around the world. Use the links provided at mezhdunami.dropmark.com to find your answers. All of your answers should be in English.

Факт 1: Russian belongs to the group of _____ languages, which can be divided into _____ subgroups. Russian is in the group of _____ Slavic languages, along with _____, Rusyn and Ukrainian. Slavic languages are spoken in many countries of Central and Eastern Europe, including Russia, _____, _____, _____, and _____ [list any four].

Факт 2: Russian is one of the top ten most widely spoken languages in the world. There are approximately _____ million speakers of Russian in the world, including some _____ million native speakers.

There are approximately _____ million Russian speakers living in the U.S. according to the 2010 census, and over 30,000 learners of Russian as a foreign language in schools and universities.

Факт 3: Russian is one of the _____ official languages used at the United Nations along with _____
_____

Имя и фамилия: _____ Число: _____

6. <u>Познакомьтесь — это известные русские.</u> Use a Russian search engine (e.g., google.ru) to look up the famous Russians listed below. Match each name to the correct picture and short description of that person by writing the letter in the blank above the picture.

The names are listed as they would be in a Russian encyclopedia: **фамилия имя отчество**. Note that, unlike in English, there is no comma between the surname and first name.

Это известные русские мужчины (famous Russian men):

    а. Барышников Михаил Николаевич

    б. Высоцкий Владимир Семёнович

    в. Гагарин Юрий Алексеевич

    г. Ломоносов Михаил Васильевич

    д. Пушкин Александр Сергеевич

___	___	___	___	___
философ, филолог, химик, физик, поэт	поэт, актёр, певец	поэт	артист балета, балетмейстер	космонавт

© information on images at end of unit.

Между нами: Домашние задания   Урок 1: часть 3   45

Имя и фами́лия: _____ Число́: _____

А э́то изве́стные ру́сские же́нщины (famous Russian women):

а. Ахма́това А́нна Андре́евна

б. Плисе́цкая Ма́йя Миха́йловна

в. Пугачёва А́лла Бори́совна

г. Хакама́да Ири́на Муцу́овна

д. Шара́пова Мари́я Ю́рьевна

____	____	____	____	____
спортсме́нка, тенниси́стка	балери́на	поэ́т	певи́ца	поли́тик

46 Уро́к 1: часть 3 — *Между нами*: Дома́шние зада́ния

Имя и фамилия: _____   Число: _____

IMAGE INFORMATION

1.7 Упражне́ние Б. Кто́ э́то тако́й? Что э́то тако́е?
1. "Common house fly, Musca domestica.jpg" by U.S. Department of Agriculture is licensed under CC BY 2.0. Last accessed October 27, 2015. https://www.flickr.com/photos/usdagov/8674435033/
2. "Pyotr Ilyich Tchaikovsky.jpg" by Chirs Reutlinger is in the public domain. Last accessed October 27, 2015. https://commons.wikimedia.org/wiki/File:Pyotr_Ilyich_Tchaikovsky.jpg
3. "Йогурт термостатный.jpg" by lanakarban is licensed under CC BY SA 4.0 International. Last accessed October 27, 2015. https://commons.wikimedia.org/wiki/File: Йогурт_термостатный.jpg
4. "Amur (Siberian) tiger prowling.jpg" by Jim Winstead is licensed under CC BY 2.0. Last accessed October 27, 2015. https://www.flickr.com/photos/jimwinstead/78555369/
5. "Samovar.silver.jpg" by Yannick Trottier (retouched by Luigi Chiesa) is licensed under CC BY-SA 3.0. Last accessed October 27, 2015. https://commons.wikimedia.org/wiki/File:Samovar.silver.jpg
6. "Hippopotamus" by Oksmith is in the public domain. Last accessed October 27, 2015. http://commons.wikimedia.org/wiki/File:Hippopotamus-PSF-Oksmith.svg
7. "Rhodesian Ridgeback" is in the public domain. Last accessed October 27, 2015. http://pixabay.com/en/dog-ridgeback-rhodesian-ridgeback-220405/

1.10 Упражне́ние Е. Фа́кты. Собы́тия. Лю́ди.
1. "Portrait of Mikhail Lomonosov" by Leontly Miropolskiy is in the public domain. Last accessed October 27, 2015. https://commons.wikimedia.org/wiki/File:M.V._Lomonosov_by_L.Miropolskiy_after_G.C.Prenner_%281787,_RAN%29.jpg
2. "Vladimir Vysotsky" by Igor Palmin is licensed under CC BY-SA 2.0. Last accessed October 27, 2015. https://www.flickr.com/photos/igorpalmin/3272298032
3. "Portrait of A. S. Pushkin" by Orest Kiprensky is in the public domain. Last accessed October 27, 2015. https://commons.wikimedia.org/wiki/File:Pushkin_Alexander,_1827_by_Kiprenskiy.jpg
4. "Baryshnikov" by Janice Waltzer is licensed under CC BY 2.0. Last accessed October 27, 2015. https://www.flickr.com/photos/pixelpackr/12390158943
5. "Yuri Gagarin" by NASA is in the public domain. Last accessed October 27, 2015. http://www.nasa.gov/topics/history/features/gagarin/gagarin.html
6. "Sharapova at official unveiling of her Canon PowerShot Diamond Collection" by Chris Gampat is licensed under CC BY 2.0. Last accessed October 27, 2015. https://www.flickr.com/photos/chrisgampat/3118444208
7. "In Swan Lake with the Bolshoi Ballet, 1966" [Maya Plisetskaya] is a non-copyrighted publicity still. Last accessed October 27, 2015. http://en.wikipedia.org/wiki/Maya_Plisetskaya#/media/File:Maya_Plisetskaya_-_1966.jpg
8. "A. Gorenko" [Anna Akhmatova] by Nikolai Gumilyov is in the public domain. Last accessed October 27, 2015. http://commons.wikimedia.org/wiki/File:A._Gorenko.jpg
9. "Алла Пугачёва на съёмках программы ФАКТОР А (2012)" by Aleksei Yermolaev is licensed under CC BY-SA 3.0. Last accessed October 27, 2015. https://ru.wikipedia.org/wiki/Пугачёва,_Алла_Борисовна#/media/File:Алла_Пугачева_на_съёмках_программы_ФАКТОР_А_(2012).jpg
10. "Irina Khakamada" by Dmitry Rozhkov is licensed under CC BY-SA 3.0. Last accessed October 27, 2015. http://en.wikipedia.org/wiki/Irina_Khakamada#/media/File:Irina_Hakamada1.jpg

Имя и фамилия: _____   Число: _____

Уро́к 2: часть 1

2.1 Упражне́ние А. Кто есть у вас в семье́? (Who Is in Your Family?)
Review the episode and place a check mark in the column labeled "Denis" if he has the relative(s) listed. Place a check mark in the column labeled "Me" if you have that relative.

	Denis		Me
1.	____	сестра́	____
2.	____	брат	____
3.	____	дя́дя	____
4.	____	бра́тья	____
5.	____	тётя	____
6.	____	сёстры	____
7.	____	де́душка	____
8.	____	де́ти	____
9.	____	ба́бушка	____

2.1 Упражне́ние Б. One, or More Than One?
Place a check mark next to the word that accurately reflects how many of each type of relative Denis has. The forms are listed in no particular order, so be careful to notice which forms are plural and which are singular.

Denis's relatives include his...

1.	____ сестра́	____ сёстры
2.	____ дя́дя	____ дя́ди
3.	____ тёти	____ тётя
4.	____ двою́родные сёстры	____ двою́родная сестра́
5.	____ двою́родный брат	____ двою́родные бра́тья
6.	____ ба́бушки	____ ба́бушка

Между нами: Дома́шние зада́ния

Имя и фамилия: _____ Число: _____

2.1 Упражнéние B. Нóвые словá

As we saw in Denis' description of his family, you can point out relatives in a family photo using **э́то** (this is). Complete each sentence below by providing a clause with **э́то** that identifies the same relationship, but for a person of the opposite gender. Use the same possessive pronoun in both parts of your sentence, but change the grammatical ending in the second half so that its matches the gender of the new noun. Notice that all of your sentences feature contrasts, so the second half will begin with the conjunction **a**. The first one has been done for you.

0. Э́то моя́ ма́ма, _____а э́то мой па́па_____.
1. Э́то на́ша ба́бушка, _____.
2. Э́то их сестра́, _____.
3. Э́то наш сын, _____.
4. Э́то наш дя́дя, _____.
5. Э́то ва́ша вну́чка, _____.
6. Э́то мой двою́родный брат, _____.
7. Э́то их оте́ц, _____.

For the remaining exercises on episode 2.1, you will need to refer to this diagram of Natalya Mikhailovna's family tree.

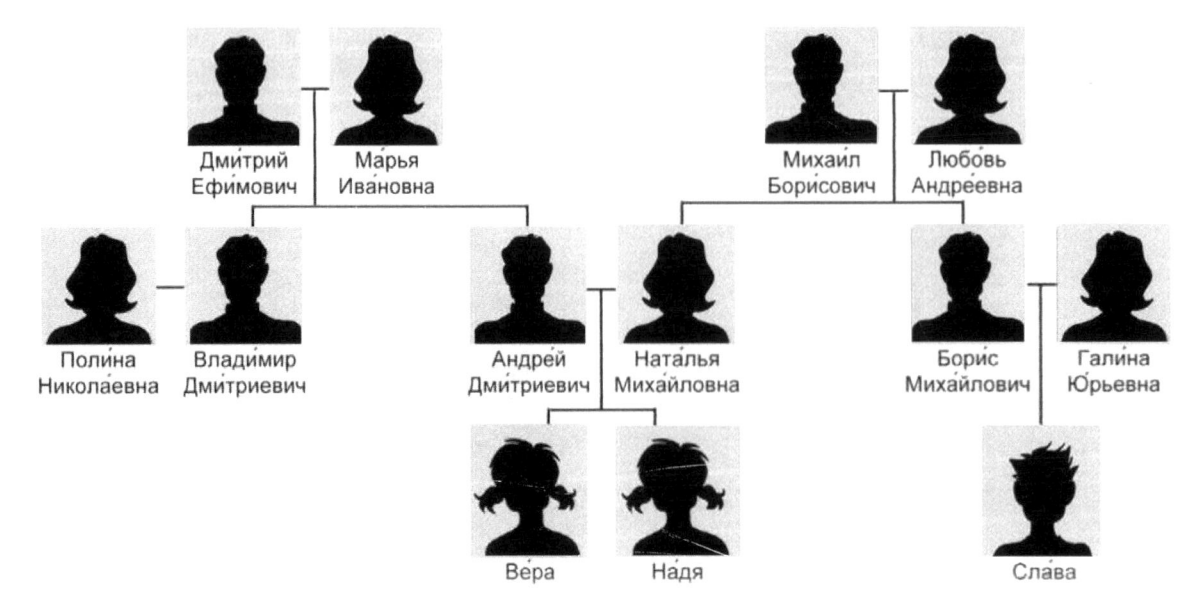

Дми́трий Ефи́мович — Ма́рья Ива́новна   Михаи́л Бори́сович — Любо́вь Андре́евна

Поли́на Никола́евна — Влади́мир Дми́триевич   Андре́й Дми́триевич — Ната́лья Миха́йловна   Бори́с Миха́йлович — Гали́на Ю́рьевна

Ве́ра   На́дя   Сла́ва

Имя и фамилия: _____ Число: _____

2.1 Упражнéние Г. Натáлья Михáйловна и её семья́

Members of Natalya Mikhailovna's family are presented below in pairs. Assume that you are the first person and then state your relationship to the second person. Write a full sentence in Russian. The first one has been done for you.

0. Нáдя / Натáлья Михáйловна

    Это моя́ мать.

1. Слáва / Борúс Михáйлович

    _____

2. Натáлья Михáйловна / Андрéй Дмúтриевич

    _____

3. Вéра / Нáдя

    _____

4. Андрéй Дмúтриевич / Владúмир Дмúтриевич

    _____

5. Мáрья Ивáновна / Вéра

    _____

6. Слáва / Михаúл Борúсович

    _____

7. Вéра / Борúс Михáйлович

    _____

8. Нáдя / Полúна Николáевна

    _____

9. Дмúтрий Ефúмович / Мáрья Ивáновна

    _____

10. Нáдя / Любóвь Андрéевна

    _____

11. Любóвь Андрéевна / Слáва

    _____

Имя и фамилия: _____ Число: _____

2.1 Упражнéние Д. Family Relationships

Look at Natalya Mikhailovna's family tree and indicate the relationship between the pairs listed below. Are they husband and wife (**муж и женá**), brother and sister (**брат и сестрá**) or some other relationship? There may be more than one way to fill in the blank.

1. Михаи́л Бори́сович и Любо́вь Андре́евна — _____.
2. Ната́лья Миха́йловна и Бори́с Миха́йлович — _____.
3. Влади́мир Дми́триевич и Поли́на Никола́евна — _____.
4. Бори́с Миха́йлович и Сла́ва — _____.
5. Ма́рья Ива́новна и На́дя — _____.
6. Ната́лья Миха́йловна и Ве́ра — _____.

2.1 Упражнéние Е. Plural Forms of Family Members

Use Natalya Mikhailovna's family tree as a guide to fill in the blanks with the appropriate family relationships. Note the changes in point of view.

1. Влади́мир Дми́триевич и Андре́й Дми́триевич — _____. Поли́на Никола́евна и Ната́лья Миха́йловна — их _____.

2. Ма́рья Ива́новна: Влади́мир Дми́триевич и Андре́й Дми́триевич — мои́ _____.

3. Ната́лья Миха́йловна: Ве́ра и На́дя — мои́ _____.

4. Ве́ра и На́дя — _____.

5. Ната́лья Миха́йловна и Поли́на Никола́евна: Влади́мир Дми́триевич и Андре́й Дми́триевич — на́ши _____.

6. Ве́ра, На́дя, и Сла́ва — _____, а Ната́лья Миха́йловна, Андре́й Дми́триевич, Бори́с Миха́йлович и Гали́на Ю́рьевна — их _____.

Имя и фамилия: _____   Число: _____

2.2 Упражнéние А. «Тóни éдет в Ярослáвль»

Match the beginning of each sentence with an appropriate conclusion so that the completed sentence reflects information from this episode.

____ 1. Вот красúвый дом,…   а. а шкóльница.

____ 2. Ярослáвль — не óчень большóй,…   б. мой дя́дя и тётя.

____ 3. Вот вся моя́ семья́:…   в. спортсмéн.

____ 4. Лúза — не студéнтка,…   г. семья́!

____ 5. Э́то моя́ сестрá,…   д. где живёт моя́ бáбушка.

____ 6. Э́то Нáстя. Её родúтели —…   е. и не óчень мáленький.

____ 7. Мой двою́родный брат Макс —…   ж. её зовýт Лúза.

____ 8. Вот э́то да! Какáя большáя…   з. родúтели, брáтья, сёстры, дя́ди, тёти и их дéти.

2.2 Упражнéние Б. Текст «Тóни éдет в Ярослáвль»

Review this episode and complete the summary below by filling in the blanks with words from the word bank. There are two extra words. You do not need to change the form of any of the words. Write in cursive.

внук	фамúлия	дéдушка	дя́дя
семья́	гóрод	млáдшая	úмя

Кто э́то? Э́то Денúс Гýрин и его́ _____. Здесь его́ родúтели и его́ _____ сестрá Лúза. А вот его́ _____ Ю́рий. Он худóжник. Тóни дýмает, что (thinks that) Елизавéта óчень красúвое _____.

А вот Зóя Степáновна. Её _____ тóже Гýрина. Она́ и Денúс — бáбушка и _____.

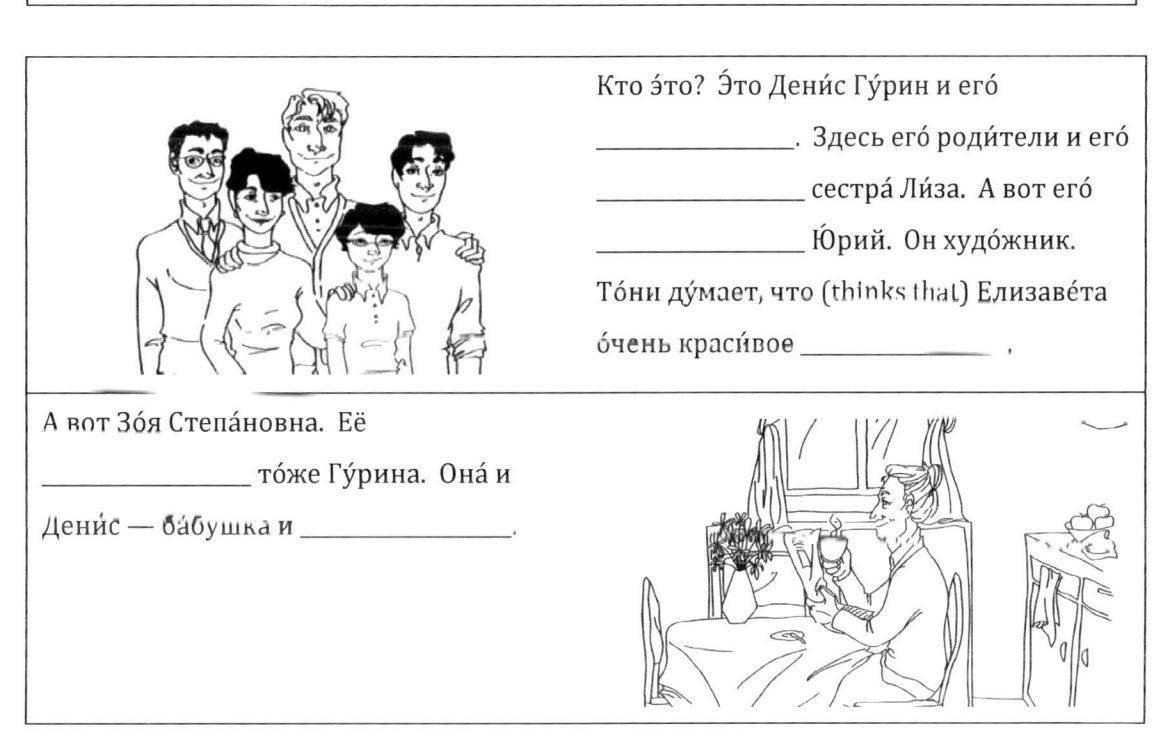

Мéжду нáми: Домáшние задáния   Урóк 2: часть 1

Имя и фамилия: _____   Число: _____

🎧 2.2 Упражне́ние В. Вот на́ша семья́

Listen to the description of the Russian family below and label each person, listing their names and whatever else you find out about them. Write your information in Russian and in cursive.

Имя и фамилия: _____   Число: _____

2.2 Упражнéние Г. Сою́зы (Conjunctions)

Select the conjunction that best fits each sentence. Then indicate whether the sentence is true or false based on the story as we know it thus far.

Sentences	True	False
1. Джош [**и** / **а** / **но**] Кéйтлин — америкáнцы.	____	____
2. Яросла́вль — ма́ленький [**и** / **а**] некраси́вый го́род.	____	____
3. Елéна Никола́евна Гу́рина — мать [**и** / **а** / **но**] женá.	____	____
4. Макс [**и** / **а** / **но**] На́стя — муж [**и** / **а** / **но**] женá.	____	____
5. Э́то То́ни. Изабéль — его́ ста́ршая сестра́, [**и** / **а** / **но**] Са́ндра — его́ мла́дшая сестра́.	____	____
6. Дени́с — ру́сский, [**и** / **а** / **но**] Ама́нда — америка́нка.	____	____
7. Вот Зо́я Степа́новна. Её дом ста́рый, [**а** / **но**] краси́вый.	____	____
8. Ната́лья Миха́йловна: «Что вы, Кéйтлин! Э́то не катастро́фа, [**и** / **а** / **но**] э́то пробле́ма.»	____	____

🎧 2.3 Упражнéние А. Вот мой дома́шний áдрес

Listen as Natalya Mikhailovna gives Caitlin her contact information and fill in the blanks with the missing words and numbers. Write all numbers as numerals. Review the numbers from 1-39 before listening.

Кéйтлин, вот мой дома́шний а́дрес:

_____ Покро́вка, _____ ____, ко́рпус ____ , _____ ____

тел. + ____ ____ ____ ____ ____ ____ ____ ____

моб. + ____ ____ ____ ____ ____ ____ ____ ____ ____ ____

Имя и фамилия: _____ Число: _____

2.3 Упражнéние Б. Нóвые знакóмые (acquaintances) и их адресá

Before Tony left for Russia, he worked as an assistant for a geography conference. The head of the geography department, Professor Jones, knows no Russian and remembers only a few random details about the Russian participants. Help Tony answer Professor Jones's questions by using the list of names and addresses below. You will write two letters in each blank.

А Петрóв Юрий Геóргиевич Ярослáвская улица, дом 15, кóрпус 4 квартира 6 Москвá	Б Андрéева Зóя Васильевна Ямскáя улица, дом 10, квартира 8 Ярослáвль
В Нóвикова Мария Олéговна Песóчная улица, дом 15, квартира 6 Владивостóк	Г Щáпова Ирина Анатóльевна Колхóзная улица, дом 51, квартира 15 Иркýтск
Д Алексéев Дмитрий Ивáнович Большáя Крáсная улица, дом 52, квартира 12 Казáнь	Е Николáев Пётр Васильевич Базáрная улица, дом 50, квартира 8 Ярослáвль
Ж Исáев Борис Михáйлович Песóчная улица, дом 11, квартира 17 Владивостóк	З Щáпова Áлла Анатóльевна Колхóзная улица, дом 51, квартира 15 Иркýтск
И Ивáнов Анатóлий Алексéевич Ярослáвская улица, дом 17, квартира 10 Москвá	

_____ Who were the two participants from Moscow?

_____ Who were the two sisters that shared an apartment?

_____ Who were the two participants that lived on the same street, but not in the same building?

_____ Who were the two participants from the same city and with the same patronymic (although they are not related)?

Имя и фамилия: _____   Число: _____

2.3 Упражнение B. Немного о наших персонажах (A Bit About Our Characters)

Fill in the information about the four characters below in cursive. For the last two lines be sure to use forms that match the gender of the character.

имя: _____   _____
отчество: _____
фамилия: _____   _____
По национальности: _____   _____
По профессии: _____   _____

имя: _____   _____
отчество: _____   _____
фамилия: _____   _____
По национальности: _____   _____
По профессии: _____   _____

Между нами: Домашние задания   Урок 2: часть 1   57

Имя и фамилия: _____ Число: _____

2.3 Упражне́ние Г. Кто они́ по национа́льности?

You are working with a multinational tour group in Russia. Look at the names of the tour group participants and try to guess what the nationality of each participant probably (**наве́рное**) is. Make sure that your guesses reflect the appropriate gender of the person. The first one has been done for you. More than one answer may be possible.

0. Pierre Beauchamp   Он, наве́рное, францу́з.
1. Marie Beauchamp   _____.
2. Hiroshi Eda   _____.
3. Noriko Eda   _____.
4. Jun Chan   _____.
5. Juan Márquez   _____.
6. Marisol Márquez   _____.
7. Günter Rolf   _____.
8. Ursula Schmidt   _____.
9. Masha Nesterova   _____.

2.3 Упражне́ние Д. Ма́ленькие слова́ и фра́зы

Review the three episodes in Часть 1 and match each English phrase with a Russian equivalent. Practice saying the Russian phrases aloud.

1. ____ What are you talking about!   а. Скажи́те, пожа́луйста.
2. ____ I know.   б. Вот смотри́те.
3. ____ I understand.   в. Спаси́бо большо́е.
4. ____ Of course.   г. Что ты!
5. ____ Please tell me.   д. Вот э́то да!
6. ____ Wow!   е. Пра́вда?
7. ____ Look here.   ж. Я зна́ю.
8. ____ Really?   з. Коне́чно.
9. ____ Thanks a lot.   и. Я понима́ю.

Имя и фамилия: _____ Число: _____

🎧 2.3 Упражнéние Е. Моя́ сестра́ то́же живёт здесь

Listen to Natalya Mikhailovna give Caitlin the contact information for her sister, who also lives in Moscow. Write all numbers as numerals.

Куту́зовский проспе́кт, _____ ____, _____ ____, _____ ____

тел. + ____ ____ ____ ____ ____ ____ ____ ____ ____ ____ ____

моб. + ____ ____ ____ ____ ____ ____ ____ ____ ____ ____ ____

2.3 Упражнéние Ж. Ситуа́ции

What Russian sentence or phrase could you say in the following situations? Review the episodes in Часть 1 if you have trouble recalling the phrases you need.

1. There is something in an ad that you do not really understand. Ask your program administrator if you can ask a question.
   _____

2. Ask your program administrator to please tell you what the thing (in the ad) is.
   _____

3. Once the administrator has answered your question, say that now you understand.
   _____

4. Ask your program administrator who your hosts are.
   _____

5. Ask your program administrator if your hosts are Russian or Ukrainian.
   _____

6. Ask your hosts if the people in a photograph are their children.
   _____

7. Compliment your hosts on what a beautiful building they live in.
   _____

Имя и фамилия: _____ Число: _____

🔍 2.3 Упражне́ние 3. Фа́кты. Собы́тия. Лю́ди. Немно́го о геогра́фии Росси́и

As our students are going to be living in different cities in Russia, you will need to have some understanding of Russia's geography, as well as some geographical terms. Watch the presentation about Russian geography and complete the following exercises.

1. Match each Russian word to its English equivalent.

    1. ____ река́   а. countries
    2. ____ города́   б. river
    3. ____ мо́ре   в. country
    4. ____ о́зеро   г. cities
    5. ____ стра́ны   д. sea
    6. ____ го́род   е. lake
    7. ____ страна́   ж. city

2. Watch the presentation again, and complete each sentence below with a Russian word from the matching activity above.

    1. Яросла́вль и Каза́нь — _____.
    2. Э́то Санкт-Петербу́рг. Там _____ Нева́.
    3. Э́то Каспи́йское _____.
    4. Э́то Ла́дожское _____.
    5. Москва́ — _____.
    6. Белару́сь и Эсто́ния — не о́чень больши́е _____.

3. Do you know the answers to these geographical riddles? Use what you have learned, and work with the maps to complete the matching activity below:

    1. ____ **река́** that flows through St. Petersburg   а. Каза́нь
    2. ____ deepest **о́зеро** in Russia   б. Украи́на
    3. ____ **мо́ре** surrounded by more than five countries,   в. Чёрное
           including Russia
    4. ____ **го́род** located on the Volga   г. Байка́л
    5. ____ **страна́** to Russia's south   д. Нева́

Имя и фамилия: _____   Число: _____

2.3 Упражнéние И. Расскажи́те о себé (Tell About Yourself)

Imagine that you are showing a Russian friend a photograph of your family. Point out each person in the photograph, stating your relationship and the person's name. You might add one more detail about each person if you already know a Russian word that fits the person (e.g., **музыкáнт**, **америкáнец**, or **дóбрый** or **интерéсный**). After introducing your family, you might also mention your city and address.

Образéц: Это мой брат. Егó зовýт Майкл. Он .... А это ...

> *Strategy tip*: Stay within the boundaries of what you know as you introduce the members of your family. Do **not** use Google translate or another such application to "write" your introductions. The chances of the computer misunderstanding your English are very high, and your composition may wind up making no sense to your reader. If you use and adjust the phrases from our story, you can create a comprehensible and informative text that will make sense to native speakers.

<u>Моя́ семья́</u>

_____

_____

_____

_____

_____

_____

_____

_____

_____

_____

_____

_____

_____

Между нами: Домáшние задáния   Урóк 2: часть 1

Имя и фамилия: _____   Число: _____

Урок 2: часть 2

2.4 Упражнéние А. Нóвые словá: квартúра
Look at the diagram of the apartment below and number ten items on the drawing. You can label pieces of furniture, rooms or architectural features. The first one has been done for you.

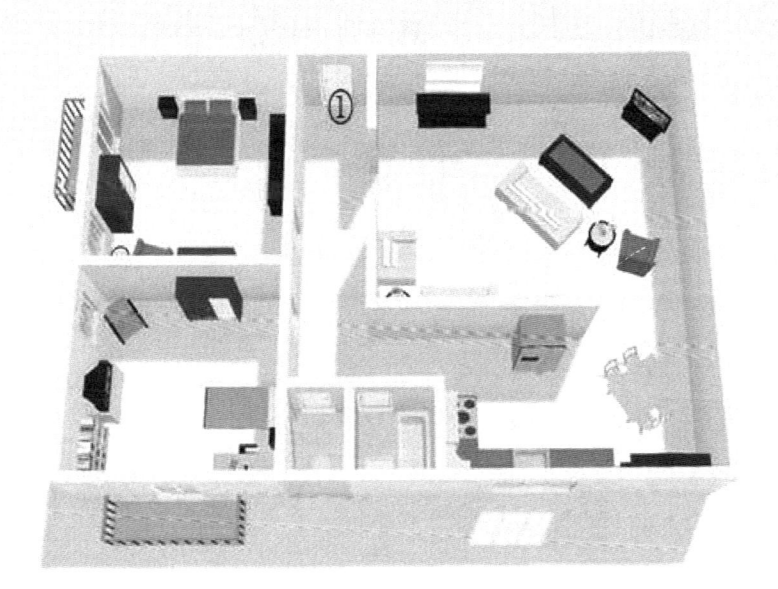

1. <u>дверь</u>
2. _____
3. _____
4. _____
5. _____
6. _____
7. _____
8. _____
9. _____
10. _____

Между нами: Домáшние задáния   Урóк 2: часть 2   **63**

Имя и фамилия: _____ Число: _____

2.4 Упражнéние Б. Живý and Its Other Forms

Nina Andreevna, who lives on a lower floor of the building, is telling Caitlin about who lives in each apartment. Complete her story and the conversation that follows it by filling in the needed forms of the verb. Pay careful attention to the grammatical subject of each verb.

Э́то наш но́вый дом. Вот кварти́ра 3, где _____ я. А ря́дом кварти́ра 4, где

_____ молода́я семья́: па́па, ма́ма и де́ти. Я не зна́ю, как их зову́т. А там

кварти́ра но́мер 5, где _____ Ири́на Петро́вна и её муж Ви́ктор Алексе́евич.

Они́ о́чень прия́тные сосе́ди.

[She spots two strangers by the door to apartment 6.]

— Э́то вы здесь _____?

— Да, мы _____ здесь. Э́то на́ша но́вая кварти́ра.

— О́чень прия́тно познако́миться. Меня́ зову́т Ни́на Андре́евна. Моя́ фами́лия Степа́нова. А как вас зову́т?

2.5 Упражнéние А. «Э́то на́ша но́вая кварти́ра»

Review this episode and complete the activities below to help you understand both the plot of the story and the meanings conveyed by specific words and phrases. In some cases you will need to find and write down exact Russian phrases used in the text, and in other cases to give their English equivalents.

1. At the end of the episode, Marat Azatovich concludes that **Ке́йтлин беста́ктная** (Caitlin is tactless). What two comments did Caitlin make that caused him to draw this conclusion? Write out the exact Russian phrases from the text.

    1. _____
    2. _____

2. Rimma Yur'evna disagrees. What is her impression of Caitlin? Fill in the Russian words/phrases that she uses on the left, and give their English equivalents on the right.

Quotation from Russian text	**English equivalent**
_____	_____
_____	_____
_____	_____

Имя и фамилия: _____   Число: _____

3. In this episode, Caitlin makes a cross-cultural discovery about some Russian apartments. What comments are made in the text? Write out the exact phrases or sentences from the text in the appropriate columns. Below each comment, give its English equivalent in parentheses.

Things said to be typical of apartments in Russia	Things said to be typical of apartments in the U.S.

4. What is Denis's reponse to Caitlin's reaction?

_____

5. Read the situations below and decide whether you would describe the participants' reaction as tactless behavior or as a normal reaction. Write out the phrase giving your opinion on the right: **Это бестáктно**. OR **Это нормáльная реáкция**.

   1. People living on the sixth floor of an apartment building are unhappy when they enter the building and see a sign saying «Лифт не рабóтает». _____

   2. A group of students has a new teacher who is around sixty. The students whisper about him in front of him, loud enough for him to hear easily: «Какóй он стáрый!» _____

   3. A Russian host has cut a guest a small piece of cake. The guest's response to the piece of cake is: «Какóй он мáленький!» _____

   4. A neighbor's cat has just had kittens. When a Russian friend sees them for the first time she exclaims «Какúе онú мáленькие!» _____

Между нами: Домáшние задáния   Урóк 2: часть 2   65

Имя и фамилия: _____ Число: _____

2.5 Упражнение Б. Как в тексте? (How Is It Said in the Text?)

Re-read the episode and choose the pair of letters that will complete the adjective + noun combination exactly as it is appears in the text. You will need to use one pair of letters twice.

ая	ое	ые
ий	ой	ый

1. Туалет маленьк_____.
2. Кухня красив_____.
3. Комната светл_____.
4. Хозяева нов_____.
5. Телевизор больш_____.
6. Телевизор стар_____.
7. Имя интересн_____.

2.5 Упражнение В. Making Adjectives and Nouns Agree

1. The left-hand column contains adjectives that already have specific endings. Only one of the nouns that follow matches the adjective in number and gender. Cross out the two nouns that do NOT match the adjective, so that you are left with a phrase in which the adjective and noun agree. The first one ("an old house") has been done for you.

0.	старый	~~кошка~~	дом	~~машина~~
1.	интересное	фото	девушки	студент
2.	красивые	комнаты	машина	американец
3.	старые	балкон	задание	родители
4.	новое	стул	стулья	сочинение
5.	интересная	семья	музыканты	президент
6.	новый	часы	кровать	рюкзак
7.	красивый	ванная	лифт	комната
8.	старая	кресло	туалет	лампа
9.	интересный	двери	окно	дом
10.	новая	дома	общежитие	кухня
11.	новые	адреса	квартира	радио

2. Now go back and consider the meaning of the phrases you have created. Circle the number of any phrases that might describe the place where you are currently living.

3. Use the blanks to write out three of the adjective + noun phrases from above in cursive. Make sure that your endings agree.

_____ _____

_____ _____

_____ _____

66 Урок 2: часть 2   *Между нами:* Домашние задания

Имя и фамилия: _____   Число: _____

2.5 Упражнéние Г. Нáши герóи (Our Characters)

Your Russian friends do not know anything about our story. Fill in the blanks with adjectives from the word bank to answer their questions. More than one adjective may be appropriate for some blanks. The adjectives in the word bank are in their **словáрная фóрма** (dictionary form), so you will need to change the endings so that the adjectives agree with the nouns they modify.

рýсский	талáнтливый	стáрый
америкáнский	хорóший	нóвый

1. — Кто такáя Кéйтлин?

    — Кéйтлин — _____ студéнтка.

2. — Кто такóй Денис?

    — Денис — _____ студéнт.

3. — Амáнда — аспирáнтка?

    — Да, аспирáнтка. Онá — óчень _____.

4. — Кто такие Джош и Тóни?

    — Тóни и Джош — _____ студéнты.

5. — Кто такáя Зóя Степáновна?

    — Зóя Степáновна — _____ хозя́йка Тóни.

6. — Ты дýмаешь, что квартира, где живёт Кéйтлин, плохáя?

    — Нет, что ты! Квартира óчень _____, и дом тóже _____.

2.5 Упражнéние Д. The Conjunctions и and но

Complete the sentences below using the adjectives in parentheses along with the conjunctions **и** or **но**. When combining adjectives you will need to think about which conjunction would best express your meaning. Remember that **и** just connects modifiers together, while **но** suggests a contradiction in expectations between the two modifiers.

Образéц: Тóни: Нáша семья́ (больш__ __ / интерéсн__ __)

Тóни: Нáша семья́ большáя и интерéсная.

1. Кéйтлин: Моя́ семья́ (óчень мáленьк__ __ / хорóш__ __).

    _____

2. Амáнда: Общежитие, где я живý, (óчень стáр__ __ / неплох__ __).

    _____

Между нами: Домáшние задáния   Урóк 2: часть 2   **67**

Имя и фамилия: _____ Число: _____

3. Денис: Наш университет (о́чень больш_́__ / интере́сн___)
   _____

4. То́ни: Го́род, где́ я живу́ до́ма, (небольш_́__ / о́чень интере́сн___).
   _____

5. Джош: Моя́ хозя́йка здесь (краси́в___ / о́чень прия́тн___)
   _____

6. Кейтлин: Кварти́ра, где́ я живу́, (но́в___ / больш_́__)
   _____

7. Кейтлин: Наш сосе́д (краси́в___ / плох_́__)
   _____

2.5 Упражне́ние Е. Personalized Sentences

Write out five sentences about yourself using the nouns and adjectives in Упражне́ние Д. When combining adjectives you will need to think about which conjunction (**и** or **но**) would best express your meaning.

Образе́ц: Наш го́род — большо́й **и** интере́сный.

Наш го́род — ма́ленький, **но** интере́сный.

1. _____
2. _____
3. _____
4. _____
5. _____

Имя и фамилия: _____ Числó: _____

2.6 Упражнéние А. «Здесь живёт Зóя Степáновна»

Complete the following summary of Tony's living situation in Russia using the adjectives in the word bank. All of the adjectives are in their dictionary forms, so you will need to change the endings to make them agree with the nouns they modify. Your paragraph should be both factually and grammatically accurate.

большóй	высóкий	интерéсный
красúвый	мáленький	небольшóй
нóвый	стáрый	ужáсный
	харóший	

Ярослáвль — _____ гóрод. Дом, где живёт Тóни, _____, но _____. Егó хозяйка — Зóя Степáновна. Её квартúра _____.

Здесь _____ потолкú и _____ óкна. Это, конéчно, плюсы. Зóя Степáновна дýмает, что _____ зéркало - не проблéма, потомý что (because) Тóни — мужчúна. Тóни дýмает, что картúна óчень _____. А сосéди и их мýзыка — _____.

2.6 Упражнéние Б. Какúе словá – онú?

Review the episode and note which nouns occur in the text in the plural, and which occur in the singular. The one word that appears in both forms has been done for you.

	singular		plural	
0.	√	потолóк	√	потолкú
1.	___	окнó	___	óкна
2.	___	сосéд	___	сосéди
3.	___	зéркало	___	зеркалá
4.	___	тýмбочка	___	тýмбочки
5.	___	кровáть	___	кровáти
6.	___	полотéнце	___	полотéнца
7.	___	шкаф	___	шкафы́

Имя и фамилия: _____   Число: _____

2.6 Упражнéние B. Plural Nouns — Regular and Irregular

Review what you have learned about making plural nouns in Russian and complete the following table. You should know all of the words in the chart.

	Singular	Plural
1.	áдрес	_____
2.	_____	балкóны
3.	_____	домá
4.	дверь	_____
5.	_____	зеркалá
6.	квартúра	_____
7.	_____	кóмнаты
8.	крéсло	_____
9.	кровáть	_____
10.	_____	кýхни
11.	окнó	_____
12.	_____	потолкú
13.	стол	_____
14.	_____	стýлья
15.	туалéт	_____
16.	тýмбочка	_____

Имя и фамилия: _____ Числó: _____

2.6 Упражнéние Г. Exclamations

Use the nouns from 2.6 Упражнéние B to complete the following exclamations and statements. Then place a check mark in the appropriate column to indicate whether the resulting phrase is more likely to be heard in a furniture store or in an unfurnished apartment. When selecting nouns for the blanks, be sure to consider the gender and number of the adjective endings.

	Furniture store	Unfurnished apartment
1. Какóй большóй _____!	____	____
2. Какáя большáя _____!	____	____
3. Это большóе _____.	____	____
4. Какие большие _____!	____	____
5. Это хорóший _____.	____	____
6. Какáя хорóшая ___ _____!	____	____
7. Какóе хорóшее _____!	____	____
8. Какие хорóшие _____!	____	____
9. Это плохóй _____.	____	____
10. Это плохие _____.	____	____
11. Это мáленькое _____.	____	____
12. Какие мáленькие _____!	____	____

Имя и фами́лия: _____   Число́: _____

2.6 Упражне́ние Д. Комплиме́нты

Tony wants to make a good impression on Zoya Stepanovna, but is a bit tongue-tied speaking Russian in front of her. Fill in the blanks to help him with a set of compliments that he could offer about her apartment. Be sure to vary your adjectives. One has been done for you.

0. <u>Кака́я</u>   <u>краси́вая</u>   ко́мната!
1. _____ _____ ку́хня!
2. _____ _____ балко́н!
3. _____ _____ дом!
4. _____ _____ о́кна!
5. _____ _____ карти́ны!
6. _____ _____ фотогра́фии!
7. _____ _____ зе́ркало!
8. _____ _____ кре́сло!

🎧 2.6 Упражне́ние Е. Кака́я э́то кварти́ра?

Strategy Tip: An important skill to develop in a foreign language is the ability to listen for the gist of what is being said, even when you do not recognize every word that you hear. In each chapter we include two or three exercises that are intentionally a bit beyond your ability to comprehend. Your task will only be to understand the text well enough to complete the tasks assigned for the passage. Your responses will be in English and will attempt to give a broad overview of the information that you hear. You may need to listen multiple times before answering the questions.

You will hear a short description of the Pavlenko family and their apartment. You are NOT expected to understand every word. Just try to get enough of what is said to complete the tasks.

The following three words may be useful as you listen:

ремо́нт = remodeling   **ря́дом** = nearby   **далеко́** = far

1. Write in the missing numerals to complete the address of the Pavlenkos' new apartment.

    Pushkin Street, house # ____, apartment # ____.

2. What are some advantages of the new apartment? List at least four, summarizing in English.
   _____
   _____

3. What are some negatives about the new apartment? List at least two, summarizing in English.
   _____
   _____

Имя и фамилия: _____ Число: _____

2.6 Упражнéние Ж. Translation

Caitlin is getting short text messages from a friend back in the U.S. who has just moved into a new apartment. Rimma Yur'evna sees her reading them on her phone and is curious what they say. Help Caitlin tell Rimma Yur'evna about her friend's apartment by translating the messages. Place a check mark next to the sentences that could also be said about the place where you live.

1. The building is big, but the apartment is small.
   _____

2. The kitchen is horrible. It is really tiny.
   _____

3. But the bedroom is large and pretty.
   _____

4. The bathroom is not bad, but small.
   _____

5. The balcony is normal, the usual.
   _____

6. The neighbors are also students. Here are [some] new photographs.
   _____

2.6 Упражнéние З. Мáленькие словá и фрáзы

Review the episodes in Часть 3 and match each English phrase with its Russian equivalent. Practice saying the Russian phrases aloud.

1. ____ And what's there?   а. наве́рное
2. ____ It works.   б. как пра́вило
3. ____ on the right   в. сле́ва
4. ____ as a rule   г. А там что?
5. ____ It's a big advantage.   д. Как э́то пи́шется?
6. ____ unfortunately   е. Он рабо́тает.
7. ____ probably   ж. Как э́то называ́ется?
8. ____ What is that called?   з. Э́то большо́й плюс.
9. ____ How is that spelled?   и. спра́ва
10. ____ on the left   к. к сожале́нию

Имя и фамилия: _____ Число: _____

2.6 Упражнéние И. Ситуáции

What Russian sentence or phrase would be said by the speaker in the following situations? Note that the situations, taken together, form a short dialogue.

1. A young woman has stopped and asked you about two buildings. You point and explain that this is the university, whereas that is the university dormitory.
   _____
   _____

2. The woman thanks you and explains that she is a new student here.
   _____

3. She tells you that her name is Anastasiya Petrovskaia.
   _____

4. You comment by saying that it is a very pretty [first] name.
   _____

5. She asks if the dorm is a good one and wants to know if you live there.
   _____

6. You explain that the dorm is okay, but you do not live there.
   _____

7. You say that your address is Kazanskaia street, house 8, apartment 4. [*Write numbers as words.*]
   _____
   _____

Имя и фамилия: _____ Число: _____

2.6 Упражне́ние К. Сочине́ние

Imagine that you are showing a visiting Russian student several photos of the place where you currently live. Write a well-organized paragraph of at least fifty words with the comments you would make while pointing to the photos. Describe the features and furnishings of your living space and give a detail or two about them. Remember to use the conjunctions **и**, **а**, and **но** to connect your thoughts. Stay within the boundaries of what you know by using the models and phrases from the story episodes and activities.

Вот [**дом** / **общежи́тие** / **кварти́ра** / **ко́мната**] [circle one], где я живу́.

_____
_____
_____
_____
_____
_____
_____
_____
_____
_____
_____
_____

Имя и фамилия: _____   Число: _____

Уро́к 2: часть 3

2.7 Упражне́ние А. Джош пи́шет блог
Match the beginning of each sentence with an appropriate conclusion so that the completed sentence reflects information from this episode.

1. ____ Дверь — чёрная, а дом —…
2. ____ Её и́мя-о́тчество —…
3. ____ Хозя́йка говори́т, что Черны́х —…
4. ____ Её маши́на …
5. ____ Его́ люби́мая ку́хня —…
6. ____ Джош — америка́нец, а…
7. ____ Его́ хозя́йка мно́го…
8. ____ Ирку́тск — интере́сный…

а. рабо́тает.
б. его́ хозя́йка — ру́сская.
в. сиби́рский го́род.
г. мексика́нская.
д. бе́лый.
е. сиби́рская фами́лия.
ж. кра́сная Тойо́та.
з. Светла́на Бори́совна.

2.7 Упражне́ние Б. Росси́я и национа́льности

а. One of the things that Josh notices about Irkutsk is the multiethnic nature of the city's population. In addition to foreigners living and working in Russia, the Russian Federation itself is home to a diverse mix of ethnic groups. Unscramble the letters and write out the names of the nationalities that Josh mentions in his blog posting.

1. еикрссу _____
2. цыкати́й _____
3. нуакицры _____
4. зукибе _____
5. аратты _____
6. тябыур _____
7. емарня _____
8. ыусролеб _____

б. Once you have unscrambled the nationality words above, match them to the names of the places below. Six of them are independent countries and two of them are regions within the Russian Federation. Mark the two regions with the letter **R**. You may need to search on the web to get more information.

1. ____ Арме́ния
2. ____ Белару́сь
3. ____ Буря́тия
4. ____ Кита́й
5. ____ Росси́я
6. ____ Татарста́н
7. ____ Узбекиста́н
8. ____ Украи́на

И́мя и фами́лия: _____ Число́: _____

2.7 Упражне́ние В. Кака́я э́то маши́на?

Think about the following brands of cars and write in the appropriate adjective of nationality. An example is given to get you started.

0. Рено́ — _францу́зская_ маши́на, а Ла́да — _ру́сская_ маши́на.

1. Ленд ро́вер — _____ маши́на.

2. Мерседе́с — _____ маши́на.

3. Шевроле́ — _____ маши́на.

4. Фи́ат — _____ маши́на.

5. Хо́нда — _____ маши́на.

2.7 Упражне́ние Г. Personalized Adjectives of Nationality

Describe the ethnic restaurants in your city by filling in the blanks below with appropriate adjectives of nationality (e.g., **америка́нский**). If your city has more than one of these restaurants, be sure to make the phrase plural. Then complete the final sentence about your food interests.

1. _____ рестора́н____   4. _____ рестора́н____
2. _____ рестора́н____   5. _____ рестора́н____
3. _____ рестора́н____   6. _____ рестора́н____

Моя́ люби́мая ку́хня — _____.

🔎 2.7 Упражне́ние Д. Вы полигло́т?

Sometimes a name in English has equivalent forms in many European languages. Look at these versions of the names John and Elizabeth, and complete each sentences below with the correct adjective of nationality. Remember that the word **и́мя** in Russian is always neuter. If you get stuck, you can consult behindthename.com.

0. John — э́то _англи́йское_ и́мя.   5. Ива́н — э́то _____ и́мя.

1. Juan — э́то _____ и́мя.   6. Elizabeth — э́то _____ и́мя.

2. Jean — э́то _____ и́мя.   7. Élisabeth — э́то _____ и́мя.

3. Giovanni — э́то _____ и́мя.   8. Elisabetta — э́то _____ и́мя.

4. Johannes — э́то _____ и́мя.   9. Isabel — э́то _____ и́мя.

Имя и фамилия: _____   Число: _____

2.7 Упражнéние E. Числи́тельные (Numbers)

Review the numbers 1-39 and then complete these math problems. Write the correct answers as numerals.

1. четы́рнадцать плюс пятна́дцать бу́дет (=) ____
2. три́дцать три ми́нус два́дцать бу́дет ____
3. двена́дцать плюс де́сять бу́дет ____
4. шестна́дцать плюс два́дцать два бу́дет ____
5. девятна́дцать плюс де́вять бу́дет ____
6. три́дцать во́семь ми́нус девятна́дцать бу́дет ____
7. шесть плюс семь плюс во́семь плюс де́вять бу́дет ____
8. два́дцать два плюс семна́дцать бу́дет ____

2.8 Упражнéние A. Ама́нда пи́шет имéйл: но́вые сосéди

Caitlin and Tony are discussing Amanda's email. Caitlin only remembers bits and pieces of the descriptions that Amanda wrote. Tony, however, has a good memory for names and can tell Caitlin whether Amanda was writing about Katya Nikolskaya, Lena Antonova or Monique Dubois. Play the part of Tony and write in the appropriate name(s) in Russian next to the word or phrase that Caitlin remembers from Amanda's email.

1. аспира́нтка   Э́то _____.
2. прия́тные де́вушки   Э́то _____.
3. францу́женка   Э́то _____.
4. сосе́дка по ко́мнате Э́то _____.
5. студе́нтки   Э́то _____.
6. хорошо́ зна́ет ру́сский Э́то _____.

Имя и фамилия: _____   Число: _____

2.8 Упражнение Б. Студенты пишут, что... (The students Write That...)

Review the episodes in Часть 3 and use the word bank to fill in the blanks in these descriptions of Josh's blog post and Amanda's email. There are three extra words. You do not need to change the form of any words in the word bank.

слева	конечно	красная
близко	белый	недалеко
красный	француженка	много
японка	только	замечательно
рядом	справа	чёрная

1. Аманда пишет, что Невский проспект _____, и университет тоже _____.

2. Джош пишет, что дом, где он живёт, _____, а дверь — _____.

3. Аманда пишет, что _____ живёт Катя Никольская.

4. Джош пишет, что его хозяйка Светлана Борисовна _____ работает.

5. Аманда пишет, что Моник, _____, не русское имя.

6. Джош пишет, что на фото (in the photo) его хозяйка Светлана Борисовна и её _____ машина.

7. Аманда пишет, что на фото Моник — _____, а Катя и Лена — _____.

8. Джош пишет, что там есть не _____ китайский ресторан, но и мексиканский.

9. Джош пишет, что всё там _____.

2.8 Упражнение В. Reviewing Adjective Endings

Misha is a pessimist, while Lyuba is an optimist who tries to convince him that things are just the opposite of what he thinks. Read Misha's pessimistic descriptions and then fill in the blanks with appropriate forms of the adjectives **хороший** and **большой** to reflect Lyuba's optimistic viewpoint. Pay careful attention the spelling rules as you write your adjective endings.

1. Миша: Комната маленькая.   Люба: Да что ты! Комната _____.
2. Миша: Общежитие плохое.   Люба: Да что ты! Общежитие _____.
3. Миша: Словарь плохой.   Люба: Да что ты! Словарь _____.
4. Миша: Машины маленькие.   Люба: Да что ты! Машины _____.
5. Миша: Полотенце маленькое. Люба: Да что ты! Полотенце _____.
6. Миша: Музыка плохая.   Люба: Да что ты! Музыка _____.
7. Миша: Рестораны плохие.   Люба: Да что ты! Рестораны _____.
8. Миша: Шкаф маленький.   Люба: Да что ты! Шкаф _____.

Имя и фамилия: _____   Число: _____

2.8 Упражнéние Г. Числи́тельные 1-199
Review the numbers 1-199 and write the numbers written out as words below as numerals.

1. со́рок во́семь _____
2. пятьдеся́т три _____
3. сто два́дцать де́вять _____
4. шестьдеся́т пять _____
5. девяно́сто де́вять _____
6. восемна́дцать _____
7. се́мьдесят четы́ре _____
8. во́семьдесят семь _____
9. сто три́дцать шесть _____
10. два́дцать семь _____
11. сто трина́дцать _____
12. пятна́дцать _____

🎧 🔍 2.8 Упражнéние Д. Адреса́: Numbers 1-199

a. Below you will find some addresses in Moscow and the surrounding region, although the house numbers are missing. Listen to the addresses and write in the missing house numbers in numerals.

1. Москва́, Профсою́зная у́лица, дом ____, ко́рпус ____
2. Москва́, Профсою́зная у́лица, дом ____
3. Москва́, Варша́вское шоссе́, дом ____
4. Москва́, Профсою́зная у́лица, дом ____
5. Москва́, Варша́вское шоссе́, дом ____
6. Москва́, Варша́вское шоссе́, дом ____ а
7. Москва́, Варша́вское шоссе́, дом ____
8. Москва́, Ле́нинский проспе́кт, дом ____
9. Москва́, Ленингра́дское шоссе́, дом ____
10. Москва́, Проспе́кт ми́ра, дом ____, ко́рпус ____
11. Люберцы́, Октя́брьский проспе́кт, дом ____
12. Люберцы́, Октя́брьский проспе́кт, дом ____ а
13. Москва́, Шоссе́ Энтузиа́стов, дом ____
14. Москва́, Шоссе́ Энтузиа́стов, дом ____

Между нами: Дома́шние зада́ния   Уро́к 2: часть 3   **81**

Имя и фамилия: _____ Число: _____

б. What is located at the addresses you just completed? What do the streets and buildings look like? Use maps.yandex.ru to search for each address and click on **Посмотре́ть на панора́ме** in the details window on the right to get a street-level view.

Look up 8 of the addresses and place a check mark in the appropriate column to indicate what you find at that location.

1. ____ shopping center   ____ apt. building
2. ____ movie theater   ____ apt. building with lots of small shops
3. ____ church   ____ post office (**По́чта Росси́и**)
4. ____ apt. building with first floor restaurant ____ school
5. ____ church   ____ Перекрёсток grocery store
6. ____ car dealership   ____ apt. building
7. ____ movie theater   ____ car dealership
8. ____ McDonald's   ____ movie theater
9. ____ restaurant   ____ school
10. ____ apt. building with book store on first floor ____ apt building with café on first floor
11. ____ church   ____ restaurant
12. ____ McDonald's   ____ bank
13. ____ bank   ____ apt. building
14. ____ hotel   ____ furniture store

в. Cultural reflection. After looking at the buildings and street-level views, what impressions do you have of these neighborhoods in Moscow? Write a few sentences in English with your observations.

_____

_____

_____

_____

Имя и фамилия: _____   Число: _____

2.8 Упражнéние E. Conjunctions: и... и / не тóлько... но и

In the box below you will find fifteen short phrases. Find two that address the same topic and that can be logically combined with the following conjunctions:

и ... , и (both ... and ...)

не тóлько ... , но и ... (not only ... , but also ...)

Not all of the phrases will combine logically (i.e., the apartment is both big and small / the car is not only new, but old) so choose carefully. You will need to re-write the original phrases to remove redundant words. The first one has been done for you.

~~кýхня большáя~~	Москвá большóй гóрод	Кéйтлин вéжливая дéвушка
маши́на мáленькая	общежи́тие нóвое	маши́на плохáя
Кéйтлин серьёзная дéвушка	Москвá краси́вый гóрод	общежи́тие большóе
общежи́тие хорóшее	кýхня стáрая	Кéйтлин бестáктная дéвушка
маши́на япóнская	Москвá интерéсный гóрод	~~кýхня нóвая~~

0. Кýхня не тóлько нóвая, но и большáя.   OR   Кýхня и нóвая, и большáя.

1. _____

2. _____

3. _____

4. _____

Имя и фамилия: _____ Число: _____

🎧 2.8 Упражнéние Ж. Нáша семья́ довóльно большáя

You will hear audio taken from a portfolio site for students studying Russian at another university. Listen and take notes in English.

The speaker's name is: _____

The speaker's siblings are: _____

_____ _____

What are three things we learn about the speaker's father?

1. _____
2. _____
3. _____

What are two things we learn about the speaker's mother?

1. _____
2. _____

The speaker mentions four people who live in Tomsk. List them below and provide at least one detail that the speaker mentions about each of them.

1. _____
   Detail: _____
2. _____
   Detail: _____
3. _____
   Detail: _____
4. _____
   Detail: _____

Имя и фамилия: _____   Число: _____

2.8 Упражне́ние 3. Познако́мьтесь, пожа́луйста! (Please Get Acquainted!)

Imagine that you are introducing the four main characters in our story to a Russian who knows nothing about our story. Write 3-4 sentences describing each of the characters. Use each of the conjunctions in the box below at least once.

a	и	но
и ..., и		не то́лько ..., но и

1. Э́то Ама́нда. _____
   _____
   _____

2. Э́то Джош. _____
   _____
   _____

3. Э́то Ке́йтлин. _____
   _____
   _____

4. Э́то То́ни. _____
   _____
   _____

Имя и фамилия: _____   Число: _____

2.8 Упражнéние И. Starting a Composition

Before starting a composition, a student wrote down some words to help describe his/her family and dorm room. Help the student turn these strings of words in their dictionary forms into sentences that make sense. You will need to conjugate the verbs, to make some nouns plural, and to make sure your adjectives agree with the nouns they modify.

1. Наш / университéт / хорóший / .

   _____

2. Вот / большóй / общежи́тие / , / where / я / жив- / .

   _____

3. Мой / кóмната / хорóший / and / удóбный / .

   _____

4. Там / стол / , / стул / , / мáленький / кровáть / and / люби́мый / чёрный / крéсло / .

   _____

5. Мой / сосéди / интерéсный / . / Они́ / канáдец / .

   _____

6. Дóма / жив- / роди́тели / .

   _____

7. Мой / стáрший / брат / — / замечáтельный / спортсмéн / .

   _____

8. Whereas / мой / млáдший / сестрá / шкóльница.

   _____

2.8 Упражнéние К. Ситуáции

A new Russian acquaintance has asked about where you are living in Russia. What sentences or phrases could you say in the following situations? Note that the sentences are connected.

1. Tell the person that your address is Novaya Street, building 20, apartment 14.

   _____

2. Explain that in your opinion the apartment is a good one. The rooms are large, and the ceilings are tall.

   _____

   _____

3. Explain that the university is not far away, and that restaurants and cafés are close.

4. Explain that your neighbors are a Russian family – a husband, wife, son and daughter.

5. Explain that they are very pleasant.

6. Explain that their son is a schoolboy, but the daughter is still little.

7. Their apartment is on the left, while yours is on the right.

8. Explain that your last name is Clinton, and that it is a common American last name.

2.8 Упражнéние Л. Сочинéние: «Моя́ семья́»

At this point in the unit you should be ready to write an essay about your own family and living situation. Remember to use language and constructions that you know, rather than trying to translate directly from English. As with all essays, a good starting strategy is to review previous exercises in the *Рабóта в аудитóрии* and *Домáшние задáния*, and to "steal" strategically from the story episodes. Write 60-75 words.

Имя и фамилия: _____   Число: _____

🔍 2.8 Упражне́ние М. Фа́кты. Лю́ди. Собы́тия. Colors and Cultural Associations

Colors are rich in associations, but those associations are often culturally specific. In this activity you will uncover some of the common Russian associations for colors, and you will compare them to associations that we have in English.

1. You already know three colors: бе́лый, кра́сный and чёрный. To find out more color words, watch the video provided at mezhdunami.dropmark.com and write down the English equivalents of the words below:

    жёлтый _____

    зелёный _____

    фиоле́товый _____

    кори́чневый _____

    ро́зовый _____

    се́рый _____

2. What are their English equivalents of the two words below?

    си́ний _____

    голубо́й _____

3. Type the word **черный** (without a ё) into the search box at yandex.ru, but do NOT hit enter! You should get a list of suggested searches that looks like this.

    The Yandex interface and the Yandex logo are registered trademarks of Yandex LLC

    a. Write the first two nouns suggested and put the English translations next to them. Your answers may differ from the ones shown above.

    _____

    _____

    б. Now do the same thing again, but use the form **чёрный**. Note any differences in the results below.

    _____

    _____

Имя и фамилия: _____ Числó: _____

    в. What results do you get for a similar search with the femine forms: **черная** / **чёрная**?

    _____

    _____

    г. What results do you get for a similar search with the neuter forms: **черное** / **чёрное**?

    _____

    _____

4. Now choose one of the colors from the beginning of this exercise and search any two of its forms (masculine, feminine, neuter, or plural). Note that си́ний has a soft **-н**, so its forms are spelled: **си́ний / си́няя / си́нее / си́ние**

    _____   _____

    _____

5. Explain the cultural significance of the following items.

    а. Чёрный квадра́т/Кра́сный квадра́т are both _____

    _____

    _____

    б. Бе́лое со́лнце пусты́ни refers to _____

    _____

    _____

    в. Ива́н Царе́вич и се́рый волк is _____

    _____

    _____

    г. Чёрный ко́фе is not just a drink, but also _____

    _____

    _____

Имя и фамилия: _____ Число: _____

6. Find out what the following items are by doing image search; if you choose to use Yandex, click on the **Картинки** link just above the search window. As you explore the images, draw lines to match each Russian phrase to its description.

бе́лая воро́на	the Russian version of Little Red Riding Hood
Бе́лая гва́рдия	the central square in the middle of Moscow next to the Kremlin
Кра́сная пло́щадь	traditionally, the corner of a Russian house where icons would be displayed
кра́сный у́гол	a crow of the wrong color --an idiom used to describe someone who doesn't fit in
Кра́сная ша́почка	a novel by Bulgakov set just after the Bolshevik Revolution and the end of World War I

7. Add any comments or questions you have about the Russian language (lexicon or grammar) or about the cultural associations you've noticed in this activity.

_____
_____
_____
_____
_____
_____
_____

Имя и фамилия: _____   Число: _____

Image Information

2.4 Упражне́ние A
   a. Room layout designed using floorplanner.com. Used with explicit written permission granted April 23, 2015.

2.8 Упражне́ние M. Фа́кты. Лю́ди. Собы́тия. Colors and Cultural Associations
   a. The screenshot of the Yandex search results are used for instructional and illustrative purposes only. The Yandex logo is a registered trademarks of Yandex LLC. https://yandex.com/company/general_info/logotype_rules/ .

Имя и фамилия: _____ Число: _____

Урок 3: часть 1

3.1 Упражнéние А. Что вы сейчáс дéлаете?
Imagine that you are the person shown in each of the pictures below and that someone has asked you the question **Что вы сейчáс дéлаете**? Write a complete sentence in cursive that answers the question. All of your sentences should start with the pronoun **я**.

1.
2.
3.
4.
5.
6.

1. _____
2. _____
3. _____
4. _____
5. _____
6. _____

🎧 3.1 Упражнéние Б. Нáстя, что ты дéлаешь?
Denis's cousin Nastya gets distracted easily, and so her mother regularly checks up on what she is doing. Listen to the questions Nastya's mother asks and fill in the missing words.

1. Нáстя, ты _____ _____ урóки?
2. Ты _____ кóмнату?
3. Ты _____, где мой журнáл «Мóда»?
4. Ты _____ рáдио?
5. Ты _____ учéбник?
6. Ты _____ сочинéние?
7. Ты _____ в доминó?

Между нами: Домáшние задáния   Урóк 3: часть 1   93

Имя и фамилия: _____   Число: _____

3.1 Упражне́ние B. Разгово́ры (Conversations)

Based on what you have learned in this episode, complete these cell phone conversations using the verbs from the word bank. The verbs should all be used in the forms in which they are given.

гуля́ю	де́лаешь	ду́маю	что
журна́л	зна́ешь	игра́ю	убира́ю
пи́шет	приве́т	рабо́таю	сала́ты

1.   Ка́тя: Ама́нда, что ты _____?

   Ама́нда: Я чита́ю _____ и пишу́ эссе́.

2.   Ке́йтлин: Джош, ты до́ма? _____ ты де́лаешь?

   Джош: Я не до́ма. Я _____ в футбо́л. А ты?

   Ке́йтлин: Я _____ в па́рке. Ты не _____, что де́лает То́ни?

   Джош: Нет, не зна́ю.

3.   Ри́мма Ю́рьевна: Мара́т, ты где? Что ты де́лаешь?

   Мара́т Аза́тович: Ри́мма, я _____, ты понима́ешь?

   Ри́мма Ю́рьевна: Ты всё ещё рабо́таешь?

   Мара́т Аза́тович: Да. А ты где? До́ма?

   Ри́мма Ю́рьевна: Коне́чно, до́ма, где же ещё? Я _____ кварти́ру.

4.   Дени́с: _____, ба́бушка, что ты де́лаешь?

   Зо́я Степа́новна: Ничего́. Я до́ма. Сейча́с де́лаю _____.

   Дени́с: Ба́бушка, То́ни сейча́с до́ма? Ке́йтлин _____ эсэмэ́ски, что она́ не зна́ет, где он.

   Зо́я Степа́новна: Он здесь, коне́чно. Я _____, что он слу́шает му́зыку.

Имя и фамилия: _____   Число: _____

3.1 Упражнение Г. Ещё о наших героях (Still More About Our Characters)

a. Tony is writing an entry in his diary about Zoya Stepanovna. He knows what he wants to say, but could use your help conjugating the verbs. You should be able to figure out the meaning of the unfamiliar words marked with ♦ by reading them aloud.

Здесь _____ Зоя Степановна. Она уже не _____. Она на
        [live]   [work]

пенсии (retired). Она _____, что её квартира старая, но очень хорошая.
                       [think]

Район — хороший, почти (almost) центр. Рядом красивый парк, где она

_____. Она _____, где магазины (stores) и поликлиника♦.
 [stroll]   [know]

Утром (in the mornings) Зоя Степановна _____ радио и _____
                                        [listen to]   [tidy]

квартиру. Потом (later) она _____ суп♦ или салаты. Иногда (sometimes)
                             [make]

она _____ письма (letters). Её дети и их семьи _____ далеко.
    [write]   [live]

б. Caitlin heard Rimma Yur'evna on Skype catching up with a childhood friend. Unfortunately Rimma Yur'evna did not speak very clearly, so Caitlin did not catch everything that she said. Help her complete the text below by filling in the missing verbs.

«Город, где мы _____, Казань. Я — школьная учительница, а мой муж
                [live]

— небольшой бизнесмен. Муж много _____. Он часто _____
                                   [work]   [write]

письма, контракты♦, документы. Я, конечно, _____ сочинения и
                                             [read]

_____ комментарии♦.
 [write]

Только в уик-энд♦ мы дома. Я _____ квартиру. Я _____ суп и
                              [tidy]   [make]

салаты. Вечером (in the evening) мы немного _____ и _____
                                             [relax]   [listen to]

музыку. Рядом большой зал♦, где мы часто _____ концерты♦. Сейчас
                                          [listen to]

здесь _____ Кейтлин, американская студентка. Мы _____,
       [live]   [think]

что Кейтлин очень хорошо _____ по-русски. Теперь она хорошо
                          [understand]

_____ центр, потому что (because) она часто там _____.»
 [know]   [stroll]

Между нами: Домашние задания   Урок 3: часть 1   95

Имя и фамилия: _____ Число: _____

в. Re-read the passages above and decide which activities the pairs of characters have in common. Remember to use the **они** form of the verbs as there is a compound subject (i.e., more than one person).

Зоя Степановна и Кейтлин _____.

Марат Азатович и Римма Юрьевна _____.

Зоя Степановна и Марат Азатович _____.

Зоя Степановна и Римма Юрьевна _____.

🎧 3.1 Упражнение Д. Кто говорит? (Who Is Talking?)

Listen and fill in the blanks to complete the sentences. Then indicate which character might say each of the statements by writing the appropriate name in the right-hand column.

	Кто это говорит?
1. Я много _____, потому что я _____.	_____
2. Я сейчас _____ музыку, а моя хозяйка _____ на кухне.	_____
3. Я _____ здесь уже месяц (for a month), и теперь я неплохо _____ Иркутск.	_____
4. _____ на фотографии и река Нева и музей Эрмитаж. Я часто здесь _____.	_____
5. Сегодня суббота. Сегодня я _____ работаю, сегодня я только _____.	_____
6. Сегодня суббота. Я _____ квартиру.	_____
7. Я _____ спортсмен. Я _____ и в футбол, и в волейбол, и в бейсбол.	_____
8. Я _____, что я неплохой бизнесмен. Сейчас я _____ большой контракт.	_____

Имя и фамилия: _____ Число: _____

3.2 Упражне́ние А. Ама́нда мно́го и́ли ма́ло рабо́тает?

Fill in the blanks with the names of the characters to accurately reflect what we learned in this episode.

1. _____ всё вре́мя рабо́тает.
2. _____ пи́шет эсэмэ́ску.
3. _____ никогда́ не отдыха́ет.
4. _____ ду́мает, что _____ о́чень серьёзная!
5. _____ зна́ют но́вый но́мер телефо́на Ка́ти.
6. _____ гуля́ют.
7. _____ ду́мает, что _____ о́чень любопы́тный.

3.2 Упражне́ние Б. Ма́ленькие слова́

Match each Russian word or phrase to its English equivalent.

____ 1. мно́го   а. simply
____ 2. ма́ло   б. in my opinion
____ 3. ведь   в. of course
____ 4. про́сто   г. hi
____ 5. по-мо́ему   д. a lot
____ 6. сего́дня   е. little
____ 7. почему́   ж. bye
____ 8. приве́т   з. why
____ 9. пока́   и. today
____ 10. коне́чно   к. after all; you know

Между нами: Дома́шние зада́ния   Уро́к 3: часть 1   97

Имя и фамилия: _____ Числo: _____

3.2 Упражнéние В. Перевóд (Translation)

Tony and Josh have been texting each other in English. Later that day Tony tells Zoya Stepanovna about their conversation and translates the text messages on his phone. How would their dialog sound in Russian? Remember that Russian does not use auxiliary verbs, so do NOT translate literally. If you are unsure about how to say things, review past episodes for help with vocabulary and word order. Do not translate the words in brackets.

Tony: Josh, what are you doing now?

Josh: I am at home. I am relaxing. And you?

Tony: I am listening to the radio. The music is very interesting.

Josh: Do you go strolling [*i.e., take walks*] a lot?

Tony: Yes, I do stroll a lot. Here [*there is*] a great park.

Тóни: _____

Джош: _____

Тóни: _____

Джош: _____

Тóни: _____

Имя и фамилия: _____ Число: _____

3.3 УПРАЖНЕ́НИЕ A. RECOGNIZING SUBJECTS AND DIRECT OBJECTS

Read the short text below about Zoya Stepanovna and one of her neighbors, and complete the following actions:

1. Find all of the verbs in the text and write the letter **г** over them for **глаго́л** (verb).
2. Draw an arrow from each conjugated verb to its subject. Underline the subject if it is more than one word.
3. Circle the direct objects of the verbs. Not every verb will take a direct object.

One verb has been done for you as a model.

Вот дом но́мер де́вять, где живёт Зо́я Степа́новна. А ря́дом дом но́мер оди́ннадцать, где живёт Тама́ра Ива́новна Соловьёва. Тама́ра Ива́новна хорошо́ зна́ет Зо́ю Степа́новну. Они́ хоро́шие сосе́дки. Тама́ра Ива́новна зна́ет, что Зо́я Степа́новна у́тром слу́шает ра́дио и пото́м чита́ет газе́ту.

Зо́я Степа́новна ча́сто пи́шет пи́сьма.

Зо́я Степа́новна непло́хо зна́ет Тама́ру Ива́новну. Она́ зна́ет, что Тама́ра Ива́новна — преподава́тель. Её специа́льность — ру́сская исто́рия. Она́ сейча́с пи́шет но́вый уче́бник. Когда́ (when) Тама́ра Ива́новна отдыха́ет, она́ чита́ет *рома́ны*. Её люби́мый рома́н — «Ма́стер и Маргари́та».

Но сего́дня — типи́чная суббо́та. Зна́чит, и Зо́я Степа́новна, и Тама́ра Ива́новна до́ма и убира́ют кварти́ру.

Между нами: Дома́шние зада́ния Уро́к 3: часть 1

Имя и фамилия: _____ Число: _____

3.3 Упражнéние Б. Кто что читáет? (Who is Reading What?)

Most of the friends that Denis had from high school have gone on to study different disciplines. Below is a list of their names and areas of interest.

Гáля — журналúстика	Нáдя — экологúя	Мúша — истóрия
Тáня — медицúна	Тóля — финáнсы	Úгорь — релúгия
Андрéй — классúческая мýзыка		Ирúна — педагóгика

a. Based on their interests, indicate which of Denis's friends is likely to be reading the items mentioned below. Write the name of the likely reader in the blank in the left-hand column to complete the sentence.

словáрная фóрма

1. _____ читáет книгу «Арáльское мóре и проблéмы экологии». _____

2. _____ читáет газéту «Коммерсáнтъ». _____

3. _____ читáет биогрáфию «Áнна Политкóвская». _____

4. _____ читáет статью «Аллергúя и иммýнная систéма». _____

5. _____ читáет журнáл «Óпера+». _____

6. _____ читáет книгу «Бýдда и буддúзм». _____

7. _____ читáет учéбник «Шкóла и дéти». _____

8. _____ читáет энциклопéдию «Совéтская Россúя: 1917-1941». _____

б. Once you have decided who is reading each item, go back and underline all the of the direct objects of the verb **читáет**. Note that the genre words (e.g., book, article, etc.) that precede the actual titles in quotes are in the accusative case. Write down the **словáрная фóрма** of the genre word in the right-hand column. While the genre words may change forms in the accusative case, the titles in quotation marks that follow the genre words do not.

Имя и фамилия: _____ Число: _____

3.3 Упражнение В. А что вы читаете, пишете, и слушаете?

What do you read, write and listen to regularly? Fill in the first part of the sentence with the appropriate verb phrase(s) to make the sentence true for you. If you do not read, write or listen to an item on the list, put a dash (—) in the blank. Be sure to make your verbs agree with their subject, which will be the pronoun **я**. Note that the direct objects in these sentences are already in the accusative case. Many of them are in the plural, since you are writing about activities that you do on a regular basis.

0. _____Я пишу_____ блог.
1. _____ книги.
2. _____ статьи.
3. _____ эссе.
4. _____ газеты.
5. _____ музыку.
6. _____ эсэмэски.
7. _____ учебники.
8. _____ романы.
9. _____ журналы.
10. _____ песни.

Между нами: Домашние задания

Имя и фамилия: _____   Число: _____

3.3 Упражнéние Г. Sentence Building

"Slash" or "dehydrated" sentences are a type of exercise that provide all the building blocks for well-constructed and meaningful Russian sentences. When you do this kind of exercise it is important that you think about the following:

- What meaning should the finished sentence convey?
- What grammar issues do I need to keep in mind?

Use the elements below to make complete, grammatically correct Russian sentences. The resulting text will be Tony's comments as his Russian friends look at photographs of his family members. Pay careful attention to the following grammar points:

- subjects of verbs should be in the nominative case.
- verbs should agree with their subjects.
- direct objects should be in the accusative case.
- adjectives should agree with their nouns in number and gender.

1. Мой / мла́дший / брат / слу́шай- / му́зыка / .
   _____

2. Мой / ста́рший / сестра́ / чита́й- / журна́л / .
   _____

3. Мой / мла́дший / сестра́ / де́лай- / уро́ки / .
   _____

4. Мой / роди́тели / отдыха́й- / здесь / .
   _____

5. Мой / бра́тья / игра́й- / в / футбо́л / .
   _____

6. Мой / дя́дя / пиш- / пе́сня / .
   _____

7. Вот / мы / и / наш / но́вый / телефо́ны / . / Мы / пиш- / эсэмэ́ски / .
   _____

8. Вот / мы / все / гуля́й- / .
   _____

Имя и фамилия: _____ Число: _____

🎧 3.3 Упражнéние Д. Студéнты и спорт

A group of students visiting from Russia is interested in the different sports teams at your school. Listen to the information that the leader of the Russian group gives you about their interests and match the Russian students to appropriate sports teams. All of the students will not find a team to match their interests, and more than one student might be interested in the same sport.

_____	1. swim team	а.	Áня
_____	2. wrestling team	б.	Волóдя
_____	3. basketball team	в.	Дúма
_____	4. volleyball team	г.	Жéня
_____	5. golf team	д.	Лéна
_____	6. tennis team	е.	Марк
_____	7. hockey team	ж.	Мáша
		з.	Пéтя
		и.	Тáня
		к.	Тóля

3.3 Упражнéние E. Asking Questions

Your teacher has told you that you will have a Russian-speaking visitor come to your class tomorrow. Come up with at least eight "yes/no" questions that you can ask the visitor about his/her interests. Since you do not know this person, you will need to use the formal form of address (**вы**) in your questions. Focus your questions on the activity words in Урóк 3. Practice saying your questions aloud, raising your intonation on the key word of your question. An example question has been provided for you.

0. <u>Вы слýшаете америкáнскую мýзыку?</u> _____
1. _____
2. _____
3. _____
4. _____
5. _____
6. _____
7. _____
8. _____

Имя и фамилия: _____   Число: _____

3.3 Упражне́ние Ж. Adjective Endings: Nominative or Accusative Case

The sentences below are complete and grammatically correct except for the missing adjective endings. Read each sentence carefully, and decide which case is needed for the adjective + noun phrase. Write the appropriate abbreviation, **N** for nominative or **A** for accusative, above the noun. Then go back and fill in the correct adjective ending. Remember that Russian word order is flexible, and that the subject may not always be at the beginning of the sentence. The first one has been done for you.

0. Там живёт но́в*ая* сосе́дка, Ни́на Петро́вна. *(N)*

1. Интере́сно, кто здесь чита́ет ру́сск____ газе́ту?

2. Мои́ сосе́дки ча́сто чита́ют америка́нск____ журна́лы.

3. «Огонёк» — популя́рн____ ру́сск____ журна́л.

4. Дени́с зна́ет, где интере́сн____ статья́.

5. Вы зна́ете но́в____ студе́нтку?

6. На́ша сосе́дка пи́шет интере́сн____ и оригина́льн____ статью́.

7. Студе́нты сейча́с слу́шают америка́нск____ пе́сню.

8. Вот на́ша ва́нная. Зе́ркало здесь небольш____.

9. На́ша хозя́йка сейча́с убира́ет больш____ ко́мнату.

Имя и фамилия: _____ Число: _____

3.3 Упражнéние 3. Pulling It All Together

Make as many complete, correct and logical sentences as you can by combining one element from each of the columns below. Be sure to make the verbs agree with their subjects and to put all of the direct objects in the accusative case.

я	читáй-	рýсская пéсня
ты	знай-	мáленькая кóмната
Джош	понимáй-	интерéсный блог
Тóни	пиш-	хорóшая кнúга
Кéйтлин	убирáй-	америкáнские ромáны
Амáнда	дéлай-	большáя квартúра
Зóя Степáновна	слýшай-	нóвое сочинéние
мы	игрáй-	интерéсная мýзыка
вы		рýсская истóрия
студéнты		«Рýсское рáдио»
аспирáнты		«Нóвая газéта»

1. _____
2. _____
3. _____
4. _____
5. _____
6. _____
7. _____
8. _____
9. _____
10. _____

Мéжду нáми: Домáшние задáния Урóк 3: часть 1

Имя и фамилия: _____ Число: _____

3.3 Упражнéние И. Ситуáции

Review the episodes in Часть 1. Then provide the Russian phrases that you would need in this conversation between you and Anya, a Russian friend of your roommate Sara. Note that all of these prompts are connected.

1. You come back to your apartment and find Anya there. Greet her.
   _____

2. Ask her what she is doing.
   _____

3. Comment on the fact that in your opinion she reads a lot.
   _____

4. Ask her if she knows where your roommate is.
   _____

5. She tells you that it is not a secret.
   _____

6. She tells you that Sara is making a Russian salad.
   _____

3.3 Упражнéние К. Сочинéние

Write a short (40-50 word) paragraph that describes your reading, writing and listening habits. Use genre words like **ромáн** and **статья́** rather than specific titles. You might also include information on the sports that you play or expand your paragraph by contrasting your reading, writing and listening habits with those of another person (e.g., a sibling, a roommate, a friend). Stay within the bounds of what you know rather than looking up new words.

Имя и фамилия: _____   Число: _____

Урок 3: часть 2

3.4 Упражнение А. Тони в университете
Review the conversation between Tony and Vladimir Georgievich. Match each item in the left-hand column with a logical response or conclusion in the right-hand column.

____ 1. Добро пожаловать в   а. библиотека.

____ 2. Извините,   б. где студенты слушают лекции.

____ 3. Говорите   в. здесь, в аудитории, номер 19.

____ 4. Вы, наверное, ещё не понимаете   г. медленно, пожалуйста.

____ 5. Вам здесь нравится?   д. наш русский юмор.

____ 6. Сейчас небольшая   е. наш ярославский Гарвард.

____ 7. Здесь аудитории,   ж. Очень.

____ 8. Ваши занятия всегда   з. с вами познакомиться.

                                     и. экскурсия.

                                     к. я не понял.

3.4 Упражнение Б. Какое слово нужно? (What Word is Needed?)
Read the following dialogs and use the word bank to fill in the blanks and complete the conversation. Note that there is one extra word.

зовут	поняла	просто
очень	поняли	рад
познакомиться	простите	рады

1. *Тони и Георгий Владимирович*

   — Вы Антонио Моралес?

   — Да.

   — Ушаков Георгий Владимирович. Очень _____ познакомиться, Антонио.

   — _____ приятно, Георгий Владимирович. Можно просто Тони.

2. *Кейтлин и Абдуловы*

   — Кейтлин, это мой супруг Марат Азатович.

   — _____, я не _____. Что такое «супруг»?

   — Мой муж.

   — Очень рада _____, Марат Азатович.

   — Кейтлин, вы американка, да?

   — Да, я американка. Можно _____ Кейти.

Между нами: Домашние задания   Урок 3: часть 2   109

Имя и фамилия: _____ Число: _____

3. *Европейский университет в Санкт-Петербурге. Общежитие.*

— Здравствуйте, мы ваши соседки. Меня _____ Аманда, а это Моник.

— Я — Катя. А это Лёна. Очень приятно.

— Мы тоже очень _____ познакомиться.

3.4 Упражнение В. Школа или университет? Какая фотография?

Below you will find possible captions for this set of pictures. Thumbnail pictures are presented here, but you can examine larger versions online at mezhdunami.dropmark.com. Write in the letters for the possible captions below the pictures. For a few pictures, more than one caption might make sense.

а. Это не студент, а преподаватель.

б. Это наша школа.

в. Это наш университет.

г. На фото наш первый класс в первый день школы. Тут ученики, а там их родители.

д. На фото наш класс, ученики группы «10-Б» и наша учительница.

е. Это очень большая аудитория.

ж. Это Московский университет.

з. Это учительница и ученики в советской школе.

и. Какой там сейчас урок?

к. На фото — я, моя подруга Надя, и наша учительница, Ольга Николаевна.

л. Какая там сейчас лекция?

Имя и фамилия: _____   Число: _____

3.4 Упражне́ние Г. Ситуа́ции

During your time abroad you meet people from many different schools and universities. How would you ask your new acquaintances these questions?

0. You ask a college student about her school.

   Како́й э́то университе́т?

1. You ask a 14 year-old girl if her teachers are good.

   _____

2. Outside a university classroom you ask a student what class it is.

   _____

3. You are touring a secondary school (i.e., grades 5 and up) and ask a woman if she is a teacher.

   _____

4. You ask a university student about a man he was talking to: Is that your teacher?

   _____

5. You ask a fellow student at the university if her classes are interesting.

   _____

6. You are touring a school and ask what grade this is.

   _____

3.4 Упражне́ние Д. Recognizing Gender and Number of Nouns Ending in -ия and -ие

Review the information about gender and number of nouns that end in –**ия** and –**ие** in this episode, and circle the adjective or possessive form that makes each of the sentences below grammatically correct. Be sure you know the **слова́рная фо́рма** of the noun before you make your choice. The first sentence has been done for you as a model.

0. Вот [**мой** / **моя́** /(**моё**)] зада́ние.
1. Где [**на́ша** / **на́ше** / **на́ши**] заня́тия?
2. Это [**но́вая** / **но́вое** / **но́вые**] аудито́рия.
3. Студе́нты пи́шут [**но́вая** / **но́вую** / **но́вые**] сочине́ния.
4. Петро́в — [**ру́сская** / **ру́сское** / **ру́сские**] фами́лия.
5. Это не о́чень [**интере́сная** / **интере́сное** / **интере́сные**] упражне́ния.
6. Этот шко́льник всегда́ пи́шет [**интере́сную** / **интере́сное** / **интере́сные**] сочине́ние.

Ме́жду на́ми: Дома́шние зада́ния   Уро́к 3: часть 2   111

Имя и фамилия: _____   Число: _____

3.4 Упражнéние Е. Какóе слóво нýжно? (What word is needed?)

Use the word bank to complete the conversations below. The words in the word bank are given in their dictionary forms, so you may need to change some of them into the accusative case to fit the grammatical context. You may also need to make some of them plural. There is one extra word.

аудитóрия	международный	упражнéние
биогрáфия	сочинéние	фамúлия
занятие		фотогрáфия

1. — Что ты сейчáс дéлаешь? Пúшешь домáшнее задáние?

   — Да, я дéлаю _____. Онó óчень трýдное!

2. — Ты студéнтка?

   — Да, студéнтка.

   — А что ты изучáешь?

   — Я изучáю _____ отношéния.

3. — А что дéлают эти студéнты? Онú читáют текст?

   — Нет, онú пúшут небольшóе _____.

4. — Кéйтлин, это _____ нóмер 12. Вáши _____ всегдá здесь.

5. — Кто это? [*pointing to a book cover*]

   — Это Никúта Сергéевич Хрущёв. Я читáю егó _____.

   — Кнúга интерéсная?

   — Не óчень, но _____ здесь óчень интерéсные.

Имя и фамилия: _____   Число: _____

3.5 Упражнéние А. "Вы говорите по-испáнски?"

The words **он** and **егó** in the statements below could, in principle, refer either to Tony or to Oleg. Based on what you have learned in this episode, indicate which of the two is more likely being described.

	Кто это?
1. Он говорит по-немéцки.	_____
2. Егó семья́ живёт в Техáсе.	_____
3. Егó брáтья и сёстры говоря́т и по-англи́йски и по-испáнски.	_____
4. Он пи́шет мáло и поэ́тому пи́шет не óчень хорошó.	_____
5. Он лю́бит языки́.	_____
6. Он смóтрит рýсские фи́льмы и слýшает рýсское рáдио в интернéте.	_____
7. Егó роди́тели говоря́т по-испáнски.	_____
8. Он дýмает, что все в Амéрике знáют испáнский язы́к.	_____
9. Он изучáет и международные отношéния, и рýсский язы́к.	_____
10. Он дýмает, что немéцкая граммáтика трýдная.	_____

3.5 Упражнéние Б. Мáленькие словá

Match each Russian word or phrase from the text to its English equivalent.

___	1. откýда	а. many people
___	2. почемý	б. difficult
___	3. навéрное	в. easy
___	4. трýдный	г. everyone
___	5. тóлько	д. great/excellent job
___	6. мнóгие	е. little, too little
___	7. молодéц	ж. not badly at all
___	8. мáло	з. only
___	9. лёгкий	и. probably
___	10. совсéм неплóхо	к. therefore
___	11. поэ́тому	л. from where
___	12. все	м. why

Между нами: Домáшние задáния   Урóк 3: часть 2   113

Имя и фамилия: _____ Число: _____

🎧 3.5 Упражнение B. Кто что изучает? (Who is studying what?)

a. Caitlin has a Russian conversation partner who does not quite understand the university system in the United States. Caitlin is trying to provide some examples, including information about friends who are studying abroad this year, but are taking or majoring in other subjects back home. Listen to the conversation and fill in the missing information.

— Кейтлин, я не понял — ты изучаешь филологию или _____?

— Да.

— Что «да»? Не понимаю.

— Что ты не понимаешь? И дома, и здесь в России я, конечно, _____ русский язык и русскую _____. Но дома я _____ и антропологию. В США это можно.

— А твои друзья (friends)? Они тоже _____ русский язык?

— Нет. Дома Сэм и Сара _____ международные отношения. Но сейчас они не в США. Сэм сейчас в Китае, он там _____ китайский язык. А Сара любит Францию, она сейчас в Париже. Там она изучает и французский язык и _____.

Моя подруга (female friend) Лора изучает американскую _____, но она _____ и испанский язык. Она сейчас в Мадриде. Но там, конечно, она не _____ американскую историю, там она изучает только _____ историю.

А Кевин в Германии, в Берлине. Он тоже историк, как Лора. В Германии он _____ немецкий язык. А дома и Кевин, и Лора _____ историю.

б. Using the information gathered above, complete this table of what Caitlin and her friends study at home, and during their study abroad experiences. Write your answers in English.

	During study abroad	At home in the U.S.
Caitlin	Russian and _____	Russian and _____
Sara	_____ and _____	_____
Kevin	_____	Economics and _____
Laura	_____ and _____	_____ History and _____
Sam	_____	_____

Имя и фамилия: _____ Число: _____

3.5 Упражнéние Г. Personalized sentences

Complete the sentences below with the verb **изучáй-** and an academic subject in the accusative case. Try to use the general academic subjects presented in the Немнóго о языкé section, even if your friends have more specialized fields. For example, at this stage of your language learning, neurobiology will be just biology. If you do need specialized words, consult your teacher.

Я _____.

Мой друг _____ _____.
              [úмя]

Моя подрýга _____ _____.
               [úмя]

Мои друзья (friends) _____ и _____ _____.
                          [úмя]   [úмя]

Здесь мнóгие (many people) _____.

🎧 3.5 Упражнéние Д. Кто что дéлает? (Who does what?)

Josh met some Russian students at a party, all of whom turned out to be doing something related to English, to the United States, or to the United Kingdom. As such, he had a hard time keeping straight what each of them was doing. It did not help that their names were similar: Anton, Artyom and Andrei. Luckily his conversation partner Nina is able to help him get the details correct. Listen to her comments and fill in the chart below in English.

	likes	watches	speaks
Anton			
Artyom			
Andrei			

Имя и фамилия: _____   Число: _____

3.5 Упражнéние Е. Нáша семья́

a. Fill in the blanks to complete this email excerpt from your keypal, who is writing about her family and their interests. Make sure the cued verbs agree with their subjects.

Нáша семья́ óчень интерéсная. Мы — э́то я, мой брат Кóля, моя́ сестрá Кáтя и нáши родители. Кóля _____ [likes] рок-мýзыку и игрáет на гитáре. Кáтя не _____ [play] на инструмéнте, но онá _____ [listens to] всё — и рок, и класси́ческую мýзыку, и джаз, и рэп. Онá всегдá _____ [says], какáя мýзыка хорóшая, а какáя плохáя. А роди́тели _____ [say], что в семьé Кóля — музыкáнт, а Кáтя — кри́тик.

Мы все óчень _____ [like] спорт и чáсто _____ [play] в тéннис вмéсте. А нáши сосéди не _____ [like] спорт. Они́ не _____ [understand], как мóжно люби́ть спорт. А наш пáпа _____ [likes] и футбóл. Он _____ [watches] все футбóльные мáтчи (games) по телеви́зору и́ли на стадиóне.

А вы _____ [like] спорт? Что вы _____ [watch] по телеви́зору?

б. At the end of her email your keypal asks what kinds of music and sports you like. Write four sentences in response to her questions.

Я _____ [like] _____.

Я _____ [like] _____.

Я _____ [like] _____.

Я _____ [watch] _____.

Имя и фамилия: _____   Число: _____

🎧 3.6 Упражнение А. Какие языки вы знаете?

а. You are at a party in the **филологический факультет**, and meet a very international group of students. Listen to the description of who speaks which languages, and write the corresponding letters after each speaker's name.

а. на хинди	д. по-итальянски	и. по-португальски
б. по-английски	е. по-китайски	к. по-русски
в. по-арабски	з. по-корейски	л. по-французски
г. по-испански	ж. по-немецки	м. по-японски

1. Кристина _____
2. Хироши _____
3. Маргарита _____
4. Жером _____
5. Джейн _____
6. Чен _____
7. Антон _____

б. Now that you have all of the information collected, figure out who at this party can talk with whom and in which language. Write in the names and languages in the blanks provided.

1. _____ и _____ говорят _____ .
2. _____ и _____ говорят _____ .
3. _____ и _____ говорят _____ .
4. _____ и _____ и _____ говорят _____ .
5. _____ и _____ и _____ говорят _____ .

Между нами: Домашние задания   Урок 3: часть 2   117

Имя и фамилия: _____ Числó: _____

3.6 Упражнéние Б. Языки́

Review the conversation that Tony and Oleg have about languages and complete the sentences below. Be sure to choose the appropriate language phrase (**по-___ски** or **___ский язы́к**) to match the verb in the sentence.

1. Тóни иузчáет междунарóдные отношéния и _____.

2. Олéг дýмает, что он не óчень хорошó говори́т _____.

3. Олéг филóлог. Он изучáет _____.

4. Олéг говори́т _____.

5. Олéг дýмает, что Тóни óчень неплóхо говори́т _____.

6. Олéг дýмает, что все америкáнцы знáют _____.

7. Тóни говори́т, что он плóхо пи́шет _____.

8. Тони говори́т, что егó брáтья и сёстры знáют _____ и
   _____.

3.6 Упражнéние В. Что за предмéт? (What Kind of Subject is That?)

Fill in each blank with an academic subject so that the sentence expresses your opinion.

1. По-мóему _____ трýдный предмéт.

2. По-мóему _____ лёгкий предмéт.

3. По-мóему _____ интерéсный предмéт.

4. По-мóему _____ вáжный (important) предмéт.

5. По-мóему _____ нетрýдный предмéт.

6. По-мóему _____ неинтерéсный предмéт.

7. По-мóему _____ полéзный (useful) предмéт.

8. По-мóему _____ нелёгкий предмéт.

Имя и фамилия: _____   Число: _____

3.6 Упражнéние Г. Студéнты и языки́ (Writing About Language Knowledge)

a. Use the elements below to make complete, grammatically correct Russian sentences. Remember to think about what meaning the finished sentence will convey and what grammar issues are involved in conveying that meaning. Pay careful attention to the use of the language expressions **по-___ски** or **___ский язы́к**.

1. Ю́ки / говор- / Japanese / . / Он / изучáй- / Spanish / .

   _____

2. Ни́на / понимáй- / Spanish / и / знай- / Portuguese / .

   _____

3. Брáйан / плóхо / знай- / German / , / но / хорошó / понимáй- / и / говор- / Spanish / .

   _____
   _____

4. Антóния / понимáй- / и / говор- / Portuguese / . / Онá / изучáй- / Japanese / .

   _____
   _____

5. Кароли́на / изучáй- / Spanish / . / Дóма / онá / говор- / French / .

   _____
   _____

6. Дóма / И́горь / говор- / Russian / . / Он / изучáй- / Portuguese / .

   _____
   _____

Имя и фамилия: _____ Числó: _____

6. Review the sentences that you created, and answer the following questions.

1. Which pairs of students should have little difficulty chatting at a mixer?

_____ and _____

_____ and _____

_____ and _____

_____ and _____

2. Which student(s) could tutor other students in a language?

_____ could tutor _____ in _____.

_____ could tutor _____ in _____.

_____ could tutor _____ in _____.

3.6 Упражнéние Д. Что они́ лю́бят дéлать?

Use the English cues in the word bank to fill in the blanks with the appropriate Russian infinitive forms. If you agree with the opinion expressed in the sentence, circle its number.

to live	to make	to play
to stroll	to study	to watch
to relax		to write

1. Натáлья Михáйловна лю́бит _____ салáты.

2. Её стáршая дочь Вéра лю́бит _____ на гитáре.

3. А млáдшая дочь Нáдя лю́бит _____ языки́.

4. Онá дýмает, что легкó _____ пéсни по-англи́йски.

5. Муж Андрéй Дми́триевич — большóй спортсмéн. Он лю́бит _____ и хоккéй и футбóл по телеви́зору.

6. Натáлья Михáйловна лю́бит _____ в Москвé (in Moscow), а её дóчери лю́бят

_____ и _____ в пáрке.

Имя и фамилия: _____ Число: _____

3.6 Упражнéние Е. Какие языки знают наши герои?

Here are the notes a U.S. program administrator jotted down about the language abilities of the students and administrators participating in the study abroad program to Russia. Using what you have learned thus far, write three short paragraphs: one paragraph each about two of the U.S. students, and one paragraph about one of the Russians.

> *Strategy tip:* Remember not to translate word for word. For example, if you want to say someone "has excellent German," you do not know that specific wording, but you do know how to say "he speaks German very well." If you need to say that someone's grammar knowledge is good, what you can say is that he knows grammar well.

Amanda Lee:	Excellent spoken Russian; reads very well and knows grammar. Good written Russian. Has spoken Chinese, but is not studying it; speaks at home, but does not read or write.
Antonio Morales:	Knows both English and Spanish very well; speaks both at home; reads Spanish but does not write well; very good spoken and written Russian. Good reading score in Russian. Knows grammar very well.
Caitlin Browning:	Knows French and Russian. Reads French well but does not speak much and has trouble understanding. Understands Russian, but not well; writing is adequate. Grammar knowledge is not very good.
Joshua Stein:	Knows English, Russian, Spanish and Hebrew. Reads Hebrew and speaks a little; speaks Russian well. Has difficulty with grammar. Knows a little Spanish, but not well.
Denis Gurin:	Russian, Ukrainian, English, Korean. Spoken English is not bad; reads and writes well. Has very good spoken Ukrainian; reads well but does not write. Studies Korean.
Oleg:	Reads German and English. Speaks and writes German very well. Spoken English is not good. Is studying German.
Georgii Vladimirovich Ushakov:	Has excellent spoken and written German; reads fluently. Speaks some English but not well; reads and writes English. Reads French.
Natalya Vladimirovna Zaitseva:	Reads English and French. Has good spoken and written English and reads very well. Reads German a little but does not speak well.

1. _____
   _____
   _____
   _____
   _____

Между нами: Домашние задания Урок 3: часть 2

Имя и фамилия: _____   Числó: _____

2. _____
_____
_____
_____
_____

3. _____
_____
_____
_____
_____
_____

3.6 Упражнéние Ж. Ситуáции

Review all of the episodes in Часть 2 and indicate what you would say in Russian in the following situations.

1. The administrator for your program in Russia is talking much too fast for you. Ask her to speak more slowly.
   _____

2. She says something that you missed entirely. Apologize for interrupting and let her know that you did not catch what she said.
   _____

3. Ask a group of new students if they like it here.
   _____

4. You hear an unfamiliar word – the Russian word "philologist." Find out what it means.
   _____

5. Compliment a friend on a job well done.
   _____

6. You are in New York, and you have walked into a shop that has a Russian sign on the door. Ask the person at the counter if Russian is spoken here.
   _____

7. Tell the person running the shop that you are happy to make her acquaintance.
   _____

8. You are just entering a theater. Ask the person at the door where the coat check is.
   _____

Имя и фамилия: _____   Число: _____

3.6 Упражне́ние 3. Your Language Abilities

Write a paragraph describing your own language abilities. Comment on your ability to speak, understand, read and write languages other than English, using at least three of the adverbs from the word bank. If you need help with vocabulary, review the conversation between Tony and Oleg to remind yourself how to express ideas related to language knowledge and studies. Be careful not to translate literally from English.

мно́го	немно́го	то́лько
ма́ло	хорошо́	совсе́м не
	пло́хо	

Уро́к 3: часть 3

3.7 Упражне́ние А. Где они́ живу́т? / Где нахо́дятся э́ти (these) города́?

Review the information in this episode and match the people/cities in the first column with the appropriate locational phrases in the second column. Make as many matches as you can.

_____	1. Ама́нда живёт...	а.	в го́роде Колу́мбусе
_____	2. Джош живёт...	б.	в Ирку́тске
_____	3. Ке́йтлин живёт...	в.	в Каза́ни
_____	4. То́ни живёт...	г.	в Калифо́рнии
_____	5. Ирку́тск нахо́дится...	д.	в Нью-Йо́рке
_____	6. Каза́нь нахо́дится...	е.	в Ога́йо
_____	7. Яросла́вль нахо́дится...	ж.	в Росси́и
_____	8. Петербу́рг нахо́дится...	з.	в Санкт-Петербу́рге
		и.	в Сиби́ри
		к.	в Татарста́не
		л.	в Теха́се
		м.	на реке́ Неве́
		н.	на реке́ Во́лге

3.7 Упражне́ние Б. Assimilation in Place Phrases

Look at the locational phrases below, and decide whether the preposition **в** is pronounced as [в] or its voiceless partner [ф]. If it is pronounced as [ф], write ф over the preposition. When you are done, write in the name of a city that is located in the place indicated. Write your city names in Russian. If you need help with city names, you might consult this list of world capitals ostranah.ru/ lists/capitals.php. Be careful! Not all the places are countries!

1. _____ в Герма́нии.
2. _____ в Калифо́рнии.
3. _____ в Перу́.
4. _____ в Беларуси́.
5. _____ в Кита́е.
6. _____ в Чи́ли.
7. _____ в Теха́се.
8. _____ в Джо́рджии.
9. _____ в Да́нии.
10. _____ в Се́рбии.
11. _____ в За́мбии.
12. _____ в Хорва́тии.

Имя и фамилия: _____ Число: _____

3.7 Упражнéние В. Вы знáете, где они́ рабóтают?

Complete the statements below with a locational phrase that indicates where each professional might work. You will need a preposition and the prepositional case form of the noun you choose from the word bank.

оркéстр	университéт	фи́тнес-цéнтр
теáтр	лаборатóрия	музéй
поликли́ника	шкóла	банк
	ресторáн	

1. Учи́тель рабóтает _____ _____ .
2. Преподавáтель рабóтает _____ _____ .
3. Официáнт (waiter) рабóтает _____ _____ .
4. Врач (doctor) рабóтает _____ _____ .
5. Банки́р рабóтает _____ _____ .
6. Гид (tour-guide) рабóтает _____ _____ .
7. Музыкáнт рабóтает _____ _____ .
8. Хи́мик рабóтает _____ _____ .
9. Трéнер рабóтает_____ _____ .
10. Актёры рабóтают _____ _____ .

3.7 Упражнéние Г. Где мóжно найти́ э́ти вéщи? (Where can you find these things?)

Brainstorm all of the places where you could find the following items, and write down locational phrases using appropriate Russian.

For example, for the word **учи́тель**, some possible locations might be:
- в шкóле
- в клáссе
- на лéкции
- на рабóте

Come up with at least four potential locations for each item. Do not forget to include the preposition. Try not to repeat any locations.

словá   _____ _____ _____ _____

учéбники   _____ _____ _____ _____

стол   _____ _____ _____ _____

_____ _____ _____ _____ _____

[your choice here]

Имя и фамилия: _____   Число: _____

3.8 Упражнéние A. Text Matrix for 3.8 Джош на урóке

Creating a text matrix for this episode will allow you to summarize what the text says and how it says it. You will first outline the information from the text by writing short bullet points in English in the left-hand column of the table below. Then you will go back to the text and find the Russian phrases to match your short bullet points. Copy these phrases from the text into the right-hand column of the table.

At first, it may seem like writing out exact phrases from the text is just busy work, but that is far from the truth. Finding exact Russian phrases and sentences to match your English summary will help you to focus on which Russian words and structures are used to encode those meanings. Doing this work thoughtfully will help you to learn new vocabulary and grammar forms at the same time.

The first table cell, which covers the topic "Josh & academics," has been done for you as a model. The first element in the second cell has also been provided so that you see how your text matrix will be structured. You should be prepared to share your text matrix in class.

Тéмы на англи́йском языкé	Фрáзы из (from) тéкста, где э́ту информáцию мóжно найти́ (to find)
Josh & academics • goes to <u>Columbia</u> • majors in _____ & _____ • year in school: • extra-curricular:	• Я учу́сь в Колумби́йском университéте.
Josh's family:	
Josh's family & academics:	

Мéжду нами: Домáшние задáния   Урóк 3: часть 3   127

Имя и фамилия: _____ Число: _____

Josh's living situation:	
Others' opinions about Josh's experience abroad:	
Josh's thoughts about his experience abroad:	

Имя и фамилия: _____ Число: _____

3.8 Упражне́ние Б. Семья́ Ста́йнов

Make complete sentences out of the elements below so that they accurately reflect information about Josh's family. Notice that the verbs in these sentences are given in the infinitive. Be sure to think about the verb's stem when you need to add personal endings.

1. Мой / ста́рший / брат / сейча́с / жить / в / Росси́я / , / в / Сиби́рь / .

2. Он / учи́ться / в / Ирку́тск / .

3. Там / он / изуча́ть / ру́сский / язы́к / и / эколо́гия / .

4. Он / писа́ть / , / что / его́ / хозя́йка / рабо́тать / в / рекла́мный / аге́нтство / .

5. Мой / мла́дший / брат / и / я / учи́ться / в / шко́ла / .

6. Я / в / деся́тый / класс / , / а / Бен / в / шесто́й / класс / .

7. Наш / па́па / рабо́тать / в / большо́й / фи́рма / .

8. А / наш / ма́ма / рабо́тать / в / городско́й / библиоте́ка / .

Между нами: Дома́шние зада́ния Уро́к 3: часть 3

Имя и фамилия: _____ Число: _____

🎧 3.8 Упражнéние В. Кто на каком инструмéнте игрáет?

a. You will hear a number of sentences about Russians who play the instruments pictured below. Write the name of the musician under the picture of the instrument that s/he plays.

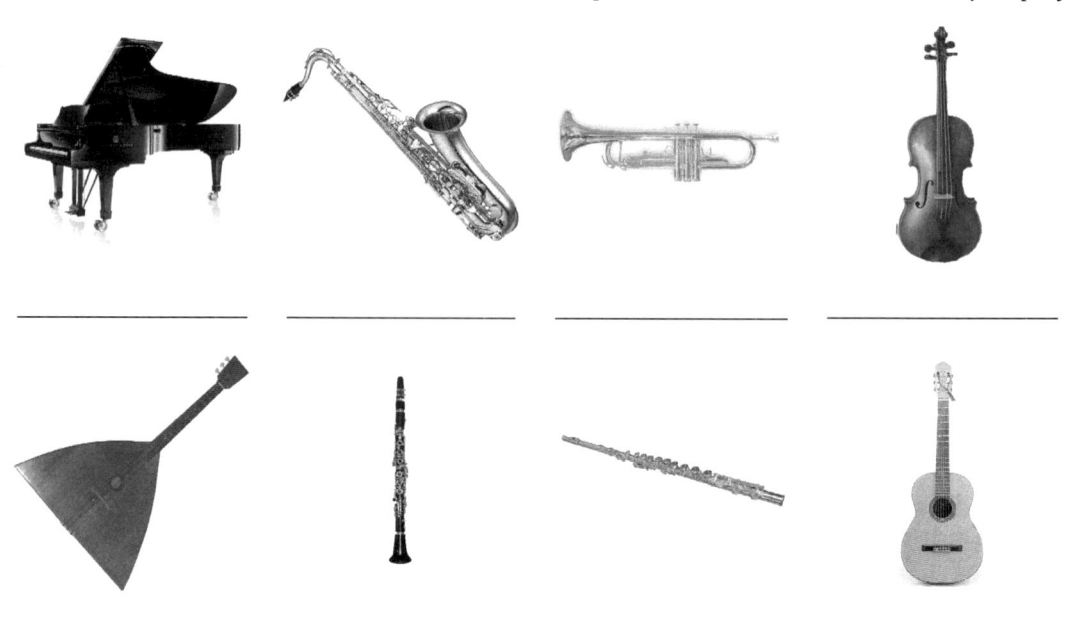

_____   _____   _____   _____

_____   _____   _____   _____

б. Answer the following questions about yourself, writing your replies in complete sentences.

1. Вы музыкáнт?
   _____

2. На какóм инструмéнте вы игрáете?
   _____

3. Вы хорошó игрáете?
   _____

4. Какую музыку вы слушаете?
   _____

Имя и фамилия: _____   Число: _____

3.8 Упражнéние Г. Studying at an Educational Institution

Use the elements below to create logical question and answer sequences. Remember to conjugate the verb **учи́ться** and to use the correct prepositional case endings on the adjective + noun phrases.

1. — Где / ты / учи́ться / ?

   _____

   — Я / учи́ться / в / Индиа́нский / университе́т / .

   _____

2. — И́горь / уже́ / рабо́тать / ?

   _____

   — Нет /, / он / ещё / учи́ться / в / университе́т / .

   _____

3. — Вы / учи́ться / в / Каза́нский / госуда́рственный / университе́т / ?

   _____

   — Нет /, / мы / музыка́нты /. / Мы / учи́ться / в / Петербу́ргский / консервато́рия / .

   _____
   _____

4. — Ваш / де́ти / ещё / ма́ленький / ?

   _____

   — Нет /, / они́ / уже́ / учи́ться / в / шко́ла / .

   _____

Между нами: Дома́шние зада́ния   Уро́к 3: часть 3   131

Имя и фамилия: _____   Число: _____

3.8 Упражнéние Д. Немнóго о себé (A Bit About Myself)

You recently met someone on the internet who speaks Russian, and you want to share some information about yourself. Complete the sentences below with locational phrases that make the statements true for you. Be sure to put the words into the prepositional case.

Remember that your new Russian acquaintance does not know much about the United States so try to express ideas in a way that will make sense to a person who has little familiarity with American culture. Use a mixture of both generic words (e.g., house, apartment, state) and geographical names (e.g., Toronto, Kansas, New York). If any of the sentences do not seem relevant to you, write a dash in the blank.

1. Я живу́ в _____ [*name of city*].
2. Наш го́род нахо́дится в _____ [*name of state*].
3. Я учу́сь в _____ .
4. Наш университе́т нахо́дится в _____ .
5. Я люблю́ де́лать дома́шние зада́ния в _____ .
6. Я люблю́ гуля́ть в _____ .
7. Мои́ роди́тели живу́т в _____ .
8. Ба́бушка и де́душка (роди́тели отца́) живу́т в _____ .
9. Ба́бушка и де́душка (роди́тели ма́мы) живу́т в _____ .

Имя и фамилия: _____   Число: _____

🎧 3.8 Упражнéние Е. Какáя кóшка вáша?

You will hear a set of sentences in which the speaker claims one item in a set of ten items. Circle the item that belongs to the speaker. The first one has been done for you.

	1-й	2-й	3-й	4-й	5-й	6-й	7-й	8-й	9-й	10-й
0.					⬤					
1.										
2.										
3.										
4.										
5.										
6.										
7.										
8.										
9.										

Между нáми: Домáшние задáния   Урóк 3: часть 3

Имя и фамилия: _____ Число: _____

3.8 Упражнение Ж. В каком классе?

After seeing some children in the courtyard playing soccer, Josh talks to one of the boys and finds out what grades they are all in. Fill in the blanks with the correct form of the ordinal number in parentheses. Remember that the dictionary form is **класс**, so you will need masculine, singular prepositional adjective endings.

Меня зовут Саша. В этой команде (team) играют Коля, Толя, Макс, Илья и я. А в другой команде играют Костя, Гриша, Петя, Паша и Федя. Федя и я учимся в _____ [5] классе. Коля и Костя учатся в _____ [6] классе. Толя учится в _____ [7] классе. Макс и Гриша учатся в _____ [8] классе, а Илья учится в _____ [9] классе. Паша учится в _____ [10] классе.

3.9 Упражнение А. Джош и его комната

Fill in the blanks to reflect Josh's point of view about the condition of his room. Note that the words in the word bank are all given in the **словарная форма** and that you may need to put some of them into other case forms to complete the text. There are two extra words.

кровать	стул	смотреть
кухня	на	Светлана Борисовна
в	говорить	тумбочка
шкаф	любить	стол

_____ думает, что я очень неаккуратный. Я не _____, когда (when) Светлана Борисовна _____ в (into) мою комнату. Она говорит, что она не понимает, почему полотенце _____ полу, книги на _____, куртка на _____, и кроссовки на _____. Она не понимает, почему большой чемодан на _____, а не на _____. А я _____ ей (to her), что это не проблема. Я всегда знаю, где всё находится.

Имя и фамилия: _____ Число: _____

3.9 Упражнéние Б. Мáленькие словá
Review episodes 3.8 and 3.9 and match the Russian words to their English equivalents.

____	1. немнóго о себé	а.	now
____	2. ещё	б.	everywhere
____	3. дóрого	в.	a bit about oneself
____	4. дáже	г.	"Good job!"
____	5. ужé	д.	still, yet
____	6. хóлодно	е.	never
____	7. тепéрь	ж.	cold
____	8. молодéц	з.	already
____	9. никогдá	и.	expensive
____	10. вездé	к.	even

3.9 Упражнéние В. Где мои вéщи?

Write at least eight sentences stating where things are located in the picture below. Remember that when objects are lying on surfaces, you will probably need to use the preposition **на** with the prepositional case to express the location. A sample sentence has been done for you.

0. Кроссóвки на коврé.
1. _____
2. _____
3. _____
4. _____
5. _____
6. _____
7. _____
8. _____

Имя и фамилия: _____   Число: _____

🎧 3.9 Упражнéние Г. Что ещё говорит Нáдя?

Nadya Antonova (whom you first met back in Урóк 2) is exchanging audio messages with Michelle, an American who is learning Russian. Listen to the latest message from Nadya and answer the questions below in English. You should not expect to understand every word in the text, but you should understand enough to answer the questions. You will need to listen to the recording three or four times, building up what you understand each time.

1. What is Nadya's address in Moscow?
   _____

2. What two details does Nadya mention about her family's apartment?
   а. _____
   б. _____

3. We know that Nadya's father is a musician. What instruments does he play?
   а. _____   б. _____

4. He has a concert on the evening that Nadya made her recording, and the program includes works by which of the following musicians:

   ____ Чайкóвский   ____ Скрябин   ____ Стравинский

   ____ Рахмáнинов   ____ Шостакóвич   ____ Шнитке

5. Where does her father perform? List at least four places.
   а. _____   б. _____
   в. _____   г. _____

6. Which of these places is his favorite? Why?
   _____
   _____

7. What are Nadya's mother's musical talents?
   _____
   _____

8. What languages does her mother know?
   а. _____   б. _____

Имя и фамилия: _____ Число: _____

9. How does her mother spend her time? List at least three activities.

    а. _____

    б. _____

    в. _____

10. What are four things that we learn about her brother?

    а. _____   б. _____

    в. _____   г. _____

11. What grade is Nadya in?

_____

12. What talent(s) does she have?

_____

3.9 Упражне́ние Д. Како́й паде́ж (What Case)?

Read the paragraphs below about an American family, and indicate the case of each underlined noun phrases by writing one of the following letters above it:

N = nominative
P = prepositional
A = accusative

На <u>фотогра́фии</u> <u>наш но́вый дом</u> и <u>моя́ семья́</u>. Сле́ва — <u>мой оте́ц</u>. <u>Его́</u> зову́т Ро́берт, и он рабо́тает в <u>шко́ле</u>. Что <u>он</u> де́лает? Он музыка́нт. Он игра́ет на <u>роя́ле</u> и немно́го на <u>фле́йте</u>. Он о́чень <u>тала́нтливый</u>.

Спра́ва моя́ <u>мать</u>. Она́ не игра́ет на <u>инструме́нте</u>, но она́ о́чень хорошо́ пи́шет. <u>Она́</u> мно́го чита́ет. <u>Что</u> она́ чита́ет? Всё! И <u>детекти́вы</u>, и <u>фанта́стику</u> (science fiction), и <u>худо́жественную литерату́ру</u>.

А ря́дом — <u>мой брат Джон</u> и <u>его́ жена́</u>. Джон — программи́ст. Он слу́шает <u>джаз</u>, но не игра́ет на <u>инструме́нте</u>. Он лю́бит <u>спорт</u>, но сейча́с он ма́ло игра́ет в <u>бейсбо́л</u>. А <u>его́ жену́</u> зову́т У́рсула. Она́ не́мка. <u>Её бра́тья</u> живу́т в <u>Герма́нии</u>, но <u>её мла́дшая сестра́</u> живёт в <u>Аме́рике</u>. <u>У́рсула</u> чита́ет <u>статьи́</u> в <u>интерне́те</u>.

Имя и фамилия: _____ Число: _____

3.9 Упражнéние E. Ситуáции

Review the episodes in Часть 3 and write out the Russian phrase that you would use in the following situations. Note that all of these prompts are connected and form a conversation between you and a teacher in Russia.

Your teacher is considerably older than you, and she speaks formally to you.

1. Your teacher in Russia asks you where you live in America.

   _____

2. You tell your teacher that you live in Vermont, in a small town.

   _____

3. Your teacher asks you at what university you study.

   _____

4. You reply that you study at Boston University (*Бóстонский университéт*).

   _____

5. Your teacher asks you what year [of study] you are in.

   _____

6. You reply that you are a second-year student.

   _____

7. Your teacher asks you if you like it here.

   _____

8. You say yes and add that your classes are very interesting.

   _____

3.9 Упражнéние Ж. Сочинéние на тéму "Немнóго о себé"

Using Josh's composition in episode 3.8 as a model, write a paragraph telling everything you can about yourself and your family. Where do you and your family members live? What music do you all listen to? What instruments do you all play? What do you all like to read and watch? What languages do you all speak and how well? At what educational institutions do you all study (if they are still students) or where do you work?

Write as much as you can, but stay within the bounds of the Russian you know. Imagine that your reader will be someone similar to Josh's teacher Irina Alekseevna, who does not live in the United States. If there are two or three Russian words that you really need in order to explain yourself to a Russian audience, make a list at the end of your composition, and your teacher will supply them.

Имя и фамилия: _____ Число: _____

IMAGE INFORMATION

3.4 Упражнéние В. Шкóла и́ли университéт? Кака́я фотогра́фия?
1. "Никольская школа, 1968 год. Выпускники 10-б" by A. Kovalevskii is licensed under CC BY 2.0. Last accessed October 28, 2015. https://www.flickr.com/photos/66851595@N04/6737399951
2. "Urban Societies In The Era Of Post-Development" by Bleb Leonov / Strelka Institute is licensed under CC BY 2.0. Last accessed June 6, 2016.
https://www.flickr.com/photos/strelka/27284074820/
3. "IMG_8728" by Kirill Kiselev is licensed under CC BY 2.0. Last accessed June 6, 2016. https://www.flickr.com/photos/115444799@N03/12722039274/.
4. "Moscow State University" by Nikolas Titkov is licensed under CC BY-SA 2.0. Last accessed October 28, 2015. https://www.flickr.com/photos/titkov/14843706652/
5. "School n2" by Vasiok1 is licensed under CC BY 2.0. Last accessed October 28, 2015. https://www.flickr.com/photos/78720675@N02/8367886040/
6. "Первая учительница" by s.lavr is licensed under CC BY 2.0. Last accessed October 28, 2015. https://www.flickr.com/photos/lavr/3880917330
7. "Лекция Тео Янсена" by Иван Гущин/Институт "Стрелка" is licensed under CC BY 2.0. Last accessed June 6, 2016. https://www.flickr.com/photos/strelka/14063481659/.
8. Untitled by Ilya Sokolov is licensed under CC BY 2.0. Last accessed October 28, 2015. https://www.flickr.com/photos/antisida/7928651150/

3.8 Упражнéние В. Кто на како́м инструмéнте игра́ет?
1. "Steinway & Sons concert grand piano, model D-274, manufactured at Steinway's factory in Hamburg, Germany" by Steinway & Sons is licensed under CC BY-SA 3.0. Last accessed October 28, 2015. http://commons.wikimedia.org/wiki/File:Steinway_&_Sons_concert_grand_piano,_model_D-274,_manufactured_at_Steinway%27s_factory_in_Hamburg,_Germany.png
2. "Tenorsax.jpg" is in the public domain. Last accessed October 28, 2015. http://commons.wikimedia.org/wiki/File:Tenorsax.jpg
3. "Trumpet 1" by PJ is licensed under CC BY-SA 3.0. Last accessed October 28, 2015. http://commons.wikimedia.org/wiki/File:Trumpet_1.jpg
4. "Violin-Viola" by Frinck51 is licensed under CC BY-SA 3.0. Last accessed October 28, 2015. http://commons.wikimedia.org/wiki/File:Violin-Viola.jpg
5. "Cello front side" by Georg Feitscher is licensed under CC BY-SA 3.0. Last accessed October 28, 2015. http://commons.wikimedia.org/wiki/File:Cello_front_side.jpg
6. "Clarinet in Eb" by Mezzofortist is licensed under CC BY-SA 3.0. Last accessed October 28, 2015. http://commons.wikimedia.org/wiki/File:Clarinet_in_Eb.jpg
7. "Guitar 1" by PJ is licensed under CC BY-SA 3.0. Last accessed October 28, 2015. http://commons.wikimedia.org/wiki/File:Guitar_1.jpg

Имя и фамилия: _____   Число: _____

Урок 4: часть 1

🎧 4.1 Упражнение А. Что у кого есть (Who Has What)?

Below each picture there are two lines. On the top line, label the object in Russian. Then listen as a Russian student tells you who in his dormitory has which objects, and write the name of the owner (or owners) in Russian on the second blank.

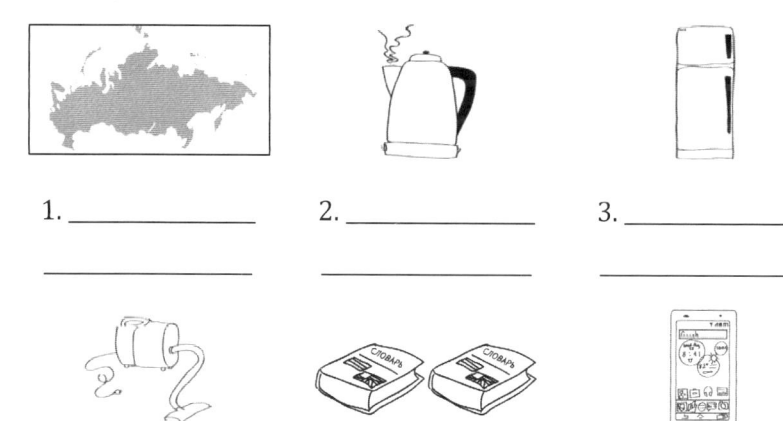

1. _____   2. _____   3. _____   4. _____

_____   _____   _____   _____

5. _____   6. _____   7. _____   8. _____

_____   _____   _____   _____

4.1 Упражнение Б. Немного о Павле

Pavel is showing you some pictures of his family and friends. Fill in the blanks so that we know what Pavel, his family, and his friends have. You will need genitive case forms of the pronouns.

Меня зовут Павел. Вот мои фотографии. Это мой брат Саша. У _____ есть японская машина. А это моя сестра Вера. У _____ есть маленькая кошка. Вот здесь на фотографии мои родители. У _____ есть большой красивый дом. Вот я на фотографии. У _____ есть сосед по комнате. Его зовут Денис. Вот мы вместе в общежитии. По-моему, у _____ отличная комната.

А вы? Что есть у _____?

Между нами: Домашние задания

Имя и фамилия: _____ Число: _____

4.1 Упражнéние В. Вопрóсы

1. Imagine that you are participating in a summer program where you will be sharing a dorm room with another Russian-speaking student. Write four questions that you would ask him/her about what he/she has. Since this will be someone your age, you can write your questions with the familiar "you."

   _____
   _____
   _____
   _____

2. Imagine that you are participating in a summer program where you will be living with a Russian host family in an apartment. Write four questions that you would ask the hosts about about what they have. For your hosts, use the formal "you."

   _____
   _____
   _____
   _____

4.1 Упражнéние Г. Нóвости из дóма (News from Home)

Caitlin has just received an email from her friend Becca about the new people she is living with in the dorms back home. Caitlin is reading the email over breakfast, and Rimma Yur'evna is curious about her news. Help Caitlin create Russian equivalents for these sentences.

1. I have a nice room.

   _____

2. I have a desk, a bed, an armchair and a small refrigerator.

   _____

3. Tom lives next door. [*In Russian your word order will be: Next door lives Tom.*]

   _____

4. He has a coffeemaker and a microwave.

   _____

5. At home, where his parents live, he has a cat and dog.

   _____

Имя и фамилия: _____   Число: _____

6. Stephanie lives on the first floor (этáж) . [*In Russian your word order will be: On the first floor lives Stephanie.*]
   _____

7. She has a new dresser and a wardrobe.
   _____

8. Megan and Laura live together in a large room.
   _____

9. They have a couch, a rug, a vacuum and a television.
   _____

10. In the dormitory, we have a washing machine.
    _____

11. But the stores are located far away. And I don't know who has a car.
    _____

4.1 Упражнéние Д. Что у меня есть?
Below are the beginnings of four sentences. Choose at least two of them and finish the sentences so that they are true for you. Think about all of the words for furniture and appliances that you know. You should name a total of 8-10 items in your sentences.

- У меня в кóмнате есть …
- У нас в общежи́тии есть …
- У меня в кварти́ре есть …
- Дóма (там, где живýт роди́тели) у меня есть …

_____
_____
_____
_____
_____

Между нами: Домáшние задáния   Урóк 4: часть 1

Имя и фамилия: _____   Число: _____

4.2 Упражне́ние A. У кого́ что есть?

Complete the table below using sentences that you find in this episode. Begin each sentence with "**у** + pronoun" or "**у** + noun" as in the examples. In the first column indicate what items the people listed have. In the second column indicate what items the people listed do not have. Copy phrases from the text exactly as you find them, and write full phrases with **есть**/**нет** rather than just objects, so that you connect the grammatical forms of the nouns to the appropriate phrases. Two sentences have been done for you as examples, but you may be able to put more information in those boxes.

	What they have	**What they do not have**
Ама́нда		У тебя́ нет ча́йника?
Мони́к		
Ама́нда и Мони́к (= мы)		
Ка́тя		
Ле́на	У Ле́ны есть холоди́льник и кастрю́ля.	
И́ра и Ма́ша		
Оле́г		

Имя и фамилия: _____ Число: _____

4.2 Упражнéние Б. Детáли, детáли, детáли

Below are the English equivalents of lines taken from this episode. Find the exact Russian from the text and write it below the English expression.

1. May I borrow your kettle?
   _____

2. I have almost nothing.
   _____

3. His room doesn't even have a lamp.
   _____

4. You also have almost everything.
   _____

5. That's all one needs.
   _____

6. There's everything there.
   _____

4.2 Упражнéние В. Есть и́ли нет?

Vera and Anton are forever contradicting each other, even when they talk about small matters. Sometimes Vera asserts that a friend of theirs has an item, while Anton is certain that the friend does not. At other times Vera is positive that their friend does not have the item they are discussing, but Anton is certain that the friend does.

1. Read the remarks below carefully. Then decide whether you need to put **есть** or **нет** in each blank. Pay careful attention to the endings on the nouns because genitive case endings indicate absence, while the nominative case endings (**словáрная фóрма**) indicate the existence of the object. That is the only way that you can tell whether the given sentence is about "having" or about "not having." You should assume that all nouns used are singular.

Вéра говори́т, что ...	**Антóн говори́т, что ...**
у Петрá Степáновича _____ смартфóн.	у Петрá Степáновича _____ смартфóна.
у Геóргия Владимировича _____ гаражá.	у Геóргия Владимировича _____ гарáж.
у Мари́ны Алексéевны _____ пылесóса.	у Мари́ны Алексéевны _____ пылесóс.
у Ли́дии Мáрковны _____ крéсло.	у Ли́дии Мáрковны _____ крéсла.

Между нами: Домáшние задáния

Имя и фамилия: _____ Число: _____

у Влади́мира Па́вловича _____ маши́ны.	у Влади́мира Па́вловича _____ маши́на.
у Серге́я Петро́вича _____ сын.	у Серге́я Петро́вича _____ сы́на.
у Людми́лы Фёдоровны _____ ковра́.	у Людми́лы Фёдоровны _____ ковёр.
у Мари́и Оле́говны _____ зе́ркало.	у Мари́и Оле́говны _____ зе́ркала.
у Евге́ния Макси́мовича и Татья́ны Евге́ньевны _____ до́чери.	у Евге́ния Макси́мовича и Татья́ны Евге́ньевны _____ дочь.
у Макси́ма Ива́новича _____ жена́.	у Макси́ма Ива́новича _____ жены́.
у Зо́и Дени́совны _____ му́жа.	у Зо́и Дени́совны _____ муж.

2. Vera and Anton are arguing about people they do not know particularly well, and so they refer to everyone using first names and patronymics. Remember that the names after the preposition **у** are in the genitive case. When names are in case forms other than the **слова́рная фо́рма**, it can be harder to recognize the person's gender.

   In the left hand margin of the table above, write the letter **М** (мужчи́на = man) or **Ж** (же́нщина = woman) above each person's name to indicate his/her gender.

3. Choose any three name-patronymic pairs from the table above, and write out their dictionary forms below. One has been done for you.

   а. ____Зо́я____ _____Дени́совна_____

   б. _____ _____

   в. _____ _____

   г. _____ _____

148 Уро́к 4: часть 1   *Ме́жду на́ми*: Дома́шние зада́ния

Имя и фамилия: _____ Число: _____

4.2 Упражнéние Г. Кóмната Мáши

a. Answer the questions below in complete sentences based on this picture of Masha's room.

1. У Мáши есть дивáн?
   _____

2. У Мáши есть кастрюля?
   _____

3. У Мáши есть холодильник?
   _____

4. У Мáши есть чáйник?
   _____

5. У Мáши есть пылесóс?
   _____

6. У Мáши есть утюг?
   _____

7. У Мáши есть микроволнóвка?
   _____

8. У Мáши есть крéсло?
   _____

9. У Мáши есть тýмбочка?
   _____

10. У Мáши есть ковёр?
    _____

Между нами: Домáшние задáния Урóк 4: часть 1

Имя и фамилия: _____   Число: _____

6. If you were subletting Masha's room with its current furnishings, what are four items you would want to acquire to make life easier? Remember to use the accusative case when completing the sentence.

   Надо купить ....

   _____ _____

   _____ _____

4.2 Упражнение Д. Светлана Борисовна и её коллеги

Svetlana Borisovna is telling Josh about some of her coworkers and friends. Turn these strings of words into complete sentences, filling in the necessary case endings.

Note: In some of the sentences **есть** has been omitted as the focus is on describing something a person is already known to have.

1. У / Вадим Петрович / большой / квартира / .

2. У / он / есть / жена / и / дети / .

3. У / Ирина Антоновна / маленький / квартира / .

4. Она / жить / одна (alone) /, / потому что / у / она / нет / семья / .

5. У / соседка / Наталья Николаевна / новый / японский / машина /, / но / нет / гараж / .

6. У / Игорь Георгиевич / старый / дом /, / но / у / он / нет / машина / .

7. У / Юлия Андреевна / новый / стиральная машина /, / но / у / она / нет / микроволновка / .

Имя и фамилия: _____ Число: _____

4.2 Упражнéние Е. Сегóдня суббóта

Imagine that it is Saturday and you are considering doing the following activities. Which ones are possible activities (**Мóжно**), which are activities you need to do (**Нáдо**), and which ones do you not want to do (**Не хочý**)? Write in one of those options before each of the phrases below.

1. _____ убирáть квартúру.
2. _____ игрáть в шáхматы.
3. _____ дéлать домáшние задáния.
4. _____ слýшать мýзыку.
5. _____ гулять в пáрке.
6. _____ читáть нóвости в интернéте.
7. _____ смотрéть телевúзор.
8. _____ игрáть на роя́ле.

4.2 Упражнéние Ж. Мáленькие словá

Match the Russian words to their English equivalents. There is one extra item in English.

____	1. давáй	а.	agreed
____	2. дáже	б.	almost
____	3. договорúлись	в.	by the way
____	4. знáчит	г.	completely
____	5. к сожалéнию	д.	even
____	6. мéжду прóчим	е.	let's
____	7. нýжно	ж.	let's go
____	8. почтú	з.	look
____	9. пошлú	и.	it is necessary
____	10. смотрú	к.	of course
____	11. совсéм	л.	that means
		м.	unfortunately

Имя и фамилия: _____ Число: _____

4.3 Упражнéние А. Жéня Кузнецóв

Match the beginning of each sentence to its logical conclusion based on this episode.

____ 1. Олéг Пáнченко —   а. в магазѝне «Эльдорáдо».

____ 2. Жéня Кузнецóв — студéнт   б. где Кáтя.

____ 3. Олéг дýмает, что   в. друг Кáти.

____ 4. Амáнда не пóмнит,   г. как называ́ется магазѝн.

____ 5. У Амáнды óчень   д. Кáти нет.

____ 6. Амáнда спрáшивает (asks),   е. на Пионéрской ýлице.

____ 7. Олéг отвечáет (answers), что   ж. не знакóмы.

____ 8. Амáнда и Жéня   з. простáя фамѝлия.

____ 9. Магазѝн «Эльдорáдо» нахóдится   и. математѝческого факультéта.

____ 10. Мóжно купѝть недорогóй электрочáйник   к. у Амáнды проблéмы.

Имя и фамилия: _____ Число: _____

4.3 Упражне́ние Б. Семья́ Ната́льи Миха́йловны

In Уро́к 2, you learned how to talk about family relationships using possessive pronouns (e.g., Liza is my sister; Elena Nikolaevna is his mother). In this exercise you will express relationships between members of Natalya Mikhailovna's family with the **'s** form (e.g., Slava is Galina Yur'evna's son). Complete the following sentences so that they reflect the relationships shown in the family tree below. Remember the **'s** form will be expressed by the genitive case in Russian. The first one has been done for you; variations are possible.

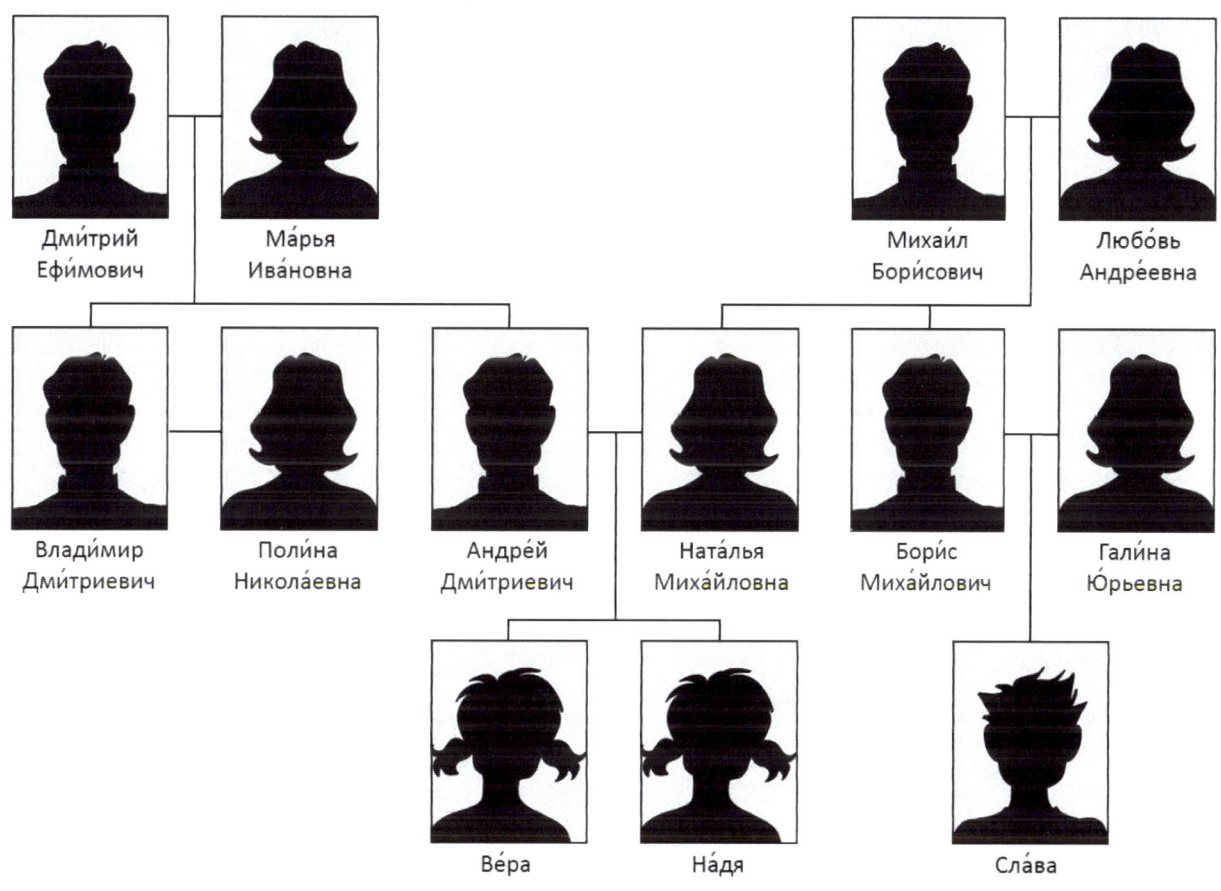

0. Гали́на Ю́рьевна — мать _____ Сла́вы _____ .
   Сла́вы is in the genitive case because Galina Yur'evna is Slava's mother.

1. Ве́ра — сестра́ _____ .

2. Поли́на Никола́евна — жена́ _____ .

3. Андре́й Дми́триевич — оте́ц _____ .

4. Бори́с Миха́йлович — муж _____ .

5. Любо́вь Андре́евна — мать _____ .

6. Сла́ва — внук _____ .

7. Гали́на Ю́рьевна — тётя _____ .

8. Ната́лья Миха́йловна — сестра́ _____ .

9. Влади́мир Дми́триевич — брат _____ .

Имя и фамилия: _____   Число: _____

4.3 Упражнéние В. Чьи э́то вéщи?

The people below are pictured with objects that they own. Write complete sentences in Russian to answer the question, "Whose object is this?" One has been done for you.

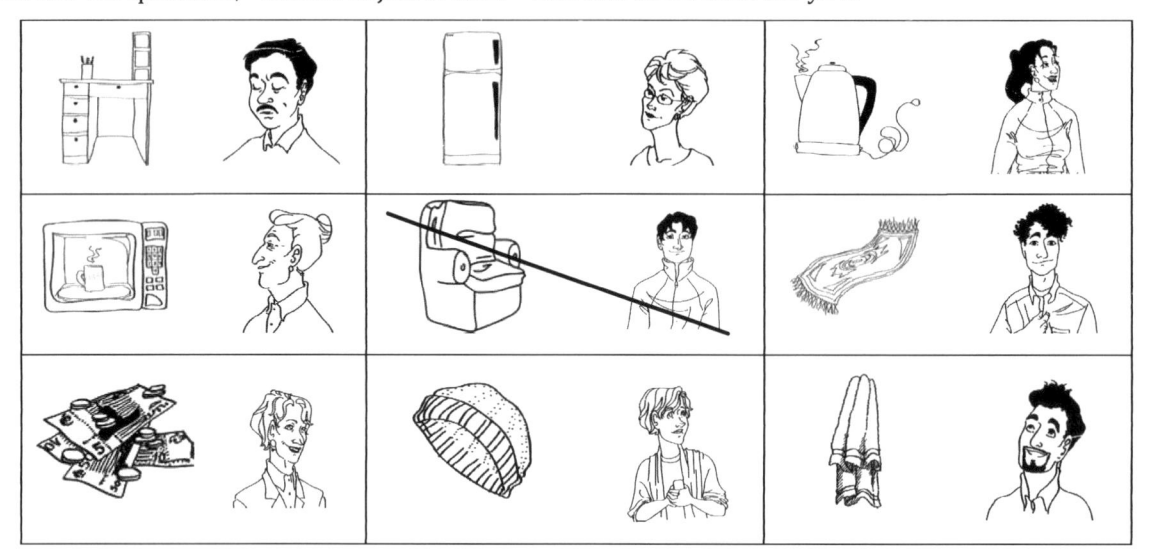

0. Чьё э́то крéсло?

   Э́то крéсло Денúса.
   Денúса is in the genitive case because it is Denis's armchair.

1. Чьи э́то дéньги?
   _____

2. Чей э́то холодúльник?
   _____

3. Чей э́то ковёр?
   _____

4. Чьё э́то полотéнце?
   _____

5. Чья э́то микроволнóвка?
   _____

6. Чья э́то шáпка?
   _____

7. Чей э́то пи́сьменный стол?
   _____

8. Чей э́то чáйник?
   _____

Имя и фамилия: _____ Число: _____

4.3 Упражне́ние Г. Моноло́г Ри́ммы Ю́рьевны

1. The sentences below form a brief monologue. All of the words are in the correct order, but the noun endings are missing. Fill in the blanks with the correct noun endings. If no ending belongs in the blank, write in ø for a "zero" ending. Think about the meaning of the sentence before you decide which case ending to use:

   - Nominative (subject)
   - Accusative (direct object)
   - Prepositional (location with **в / на**)
   - Genitive (with preposition **у** for ownership, with **нет** for absence, possessor in 's)

   Меня́ зову́т Ри́мм____ Ю́рьевн____. Я рабо́таю в шко́л____.

   Мой муж____ мно́го рабо́тает. Фи́рма муж____ называ́ется «Татарстро́й». Э́то больша́я фи́рм____.

   Я о́чень люблю́ на́шу но́вую кварти́р____. Она́ нахо́дится на у́лиц____ Кали́нина. Кварти́ра на седьмо́м этаж____. В большо́й ко́мнат____ у нас дива́н____, кре́сл____, телеви́зор____. А на ку́хн____ у нас но́вый холоди́льник____, микроволно́вк____ и но́вые сту́л____.

   В ко́мнат____ Ке́йтлин____ крова́т____, комо́д____ и пи́сьменный стол____. Там нет шкаф____, и нет вентиля́тор____. Ке́йтлин — хоро́шая де́вушк____. Она́ изуча́ет ру́сский язы́к____ и ру́сскую культу́р____.

2. When you have finished, find one example of each of the four cases listed above, and write N, A, P or G over that word or phrase.

Имя и фамилия: _____   Число: _____

4.3 Упражнéние Д. Ситуáции

Review all the episodes in **Часть** 1 and indicate what you would say in Russian in the following situations. Note that all of these prompts are connected.

1. Ask your classmate Igor' if you may borrow a pen. [*Use the accusative case for "pen."*]
   _____

2. He gives you permission, but is surprised that you do not have a pen.
   _____

3. You explain that you have a pen, but you do not know where it is.
   _____

4. While you are talking to Igor', your friend Tanya joins you. It takes you a moment to realize that Igor' and Tanya do not know each other. Apologize and comment on that.
   _____

5. Introduce Igor' to Tanya.
   _____

6. Tanya asks where one can buy an inexpensive coffee maker.
   _____

7. Igor' says that on Bolshoi Prospect [there] is a good store.
   _____

8. You tell Tanya that the store is located not far away, and invite her to head out right now.
   _____
   _____

Имя и фамилия: _____   Число: _____

4.3 Упражне́ние E. Сочине́ние: Сейча́с я живу́…

Imagine that you have set up an account on ВКонта́кте (vk.com), the Russian equivalent of Facebook. Write a post in Russian of approximately 50 words talking about where you are currently living, what kind of place it is, and what kinds of items you have there. You might also note a couple of things that you are lacking and need to buy. Begin by stating whether you live in an apartment or a dorm.

Имя и фамилия: _____ Число: _____

Уро́к 4: часть 2

4.4 Упражне́ние А. Петрогра́дская сторона́

Number the sentences below so that they reflect the order in which Amanda and Zhenya encounter things on their walk in this episode. Note there are some things that they discuss, but do not actually see on their way to the store. Place an X in the blank before those sentences. Re-read the episode carefully!

____ а. Ама́нда и Же́ня ви́дят мост.

____ б. Ама́нда и Же́ня ви́дят ста́нцию метро́ «Спорти́вная».

____ в. Ама́нда и Же́ня ви́дят бассе́йн и фи́тнес-це́нтр.

____ г. Ама́нда и Же́ня ви́дят Институ́т ру́сского языка́ и культу́ры.

____ д. Ама́нда и Же́ня ви́дят стадио́н.

____ е. Ама́нда и Же́ня ви́дят ры́нок.

____ ж. Ама́нда и Же́ня ви́дят остано́вку авто́буса.

____ з. Ама́нда и Же́ня ви́дят суперма́ркет.

____ и. Ама́нда и Же́ня ви́дят Большо́й проспе́кт.

____ к. Ама́нда и Же́ня ви́дят большу́ю це́рковь.

Имя и фамилия: _____   Число: _____

4.4 Упражнéние Б. Что это такóе?

You are a tourist in a Russian town, and the map you have uses only the small icons below to indicate places that a tourist might need to find. Look at the icons and circle the word that best represents the icon.

✚	музéй	аптéка	ресторáн	цéрковь
🏛	останóвка автóбуса	парк	аптéка	цéрковь
☕	бассéйн	стáнция метрó	кафé	туалéты
🎞	кинотеáтр	цéрковь	ресторáн	магазúн
🏊	магазúн	библиотéка	бассéйн	стáнция метрó
✉	пóчта	цéрковь	ресторáн	останóвка автóбуса
🍴	аптéка	останóвка автóбуса	ресторáн	магазúн
🏟	университéт	стадиóн	стáнция метрó	останóвка автóбуса
🏛	музéй	магазúн	парк	аптéка

🎧 4.4 Упражнéние В. Гóрод Сарáтов

You will listen to an audio post of a Russian woman talking about Saratov, her home city. Fill in the missing words in the transcript below.

Сарáтов — хорóший _____. У нас в Сарáтове есть академúческий _____ óперы и балéта и цирк. Крóме тогó (moreover), у _____ в Сарáтове недалекó от _____ Вóлги есть большáя исторúческая _____. У нас в гóроде есть и интерéсные _____. Напримéр (for example), есть Дом-музéй рýсского писáтеля _____ Чернышéвского. У нас в _____ óчень лю́бят спорт. В цéнтре есть большóй _____.

А мы живём не в _____. Но это не проблéма, потомý что рядом нахóдится _____ _____. Есть ещё одúн плюс: на нáшей _____ есть _____ и фúтнес-цéнтр. Но, к _____, есть и мúнусы. _____ нахóдится далекó от нáшего _____. Наш гóрод не óчень большóй, и поэ́тому у нас нет _____.

Имя и фамилия: _____   Число: _____

4.4 Упражне́ние Г. Есть и́ли нет?

1. During a tour of a neighborhood in Yaroslavl', Tony jotted down some quick notes. Now that he is going over them, he realizes that he cannot tell whether the items in the list were in the area or not. Fortunately he wrote down the correct grammatical form for each item. Help him out by recalling the **слова́рная фо́рма** of each noun phrase, and then writing **Есть** (nominative) or **Нет** (genitive) in the blank to match the form that Tony has on his list. All of the nouns are in the singular.

   _____ библиоте́ка   _____ па́рка

   _____ це́ркви   _____ остано́вка авто́буса

   _____ ста́нции метро́   _____ бассе́йн

   _____ апте́ка   _____ ры́нка

   _____ музе́я   _____ стадио́н

2. Would you want to live in this neighborhood? Explain briefly in English why or why not:

   _____
   _____
   _____

4.4 Упражне́ние Д. Немно́го об Алекса́ндровке

A Russian woman is telling you some things about Aleksandrovka, the small provincial city where she lives. Respond to her comments with a similar or contrasting sentence about your hometown or the city where you are studying.

You should either point out that your city also has/lacks the given feature, or point out a contrast between Aleksandrovka and your city by saying the opposite. In your responses use "**У нас в _____**," and write your city name in Russian in the correct form. Two sample answers have been given for students from Lawrence (**Ло́ренс**, which does decline) and Toronto (**Торо́нто**, which does not decline). Note the different prepositional case forms.

0. У нас в Алекса́ндровке нет теа́тра о́перы.

   <u>У нас в Ло́ренсе то́же нет теа́тра о́перы</u>   OR   <u>А у нас в Торо́нто есть теа́тр о́перы.</u>

1. У нас в Алекса́ндровке нет истори́ческого музе́я.

   _____

2. У нас в Алекса́ндровке есть филармо́ния.

   _____

3. У нас в Алекса́ндровке нет реки́.

   _____

4. У нас в Алекса́ндровке есть больша́я истори́ческая це́рковь.

Между нами: Дома́шние зада́ния   Уро́к 4: часть 2   **161**

Имя и фамилия: _____ Число: _____

5. У нас в Александровке есть большая городская библиотека.
   _____

6. У нас в Александровке есть университет.
   _____

7. У нас в Александровке есть футбольный клуб (soccer team).
   _____

8. У нас в Александровке есть очень маленький аэропорт.
   _____

9. У нас в Александровке есть драматический театр.
   _____

4.4 Упражнение Е. Моя новая квартира

Your friend Jason got an email from a Russian friend asking about his living situation. He has written a reply, but was not sure of his genitive case endings. Help him by supplying the correct genitive forms for the adjectives and nouns he wants to use.

Привет, Маша!

Спасибо за твой имейл. Ты спрашиваешь о (about) моей квартире. Я живу близко от _____ _____ и _____ _____,
[наш]   [университет]   [большая]   [библиотека]

и недалеко от _____ _____. На моей улице очень тихо (quiet):
[недорогой]   [ресторан]

нет ни (neither) _____, ни (nor) _____.
[магазин]   [остановка автобуса]

Мой дом находится далеко от _____ _____. К сожалению,
[новое]   [общежитие]

я живу далеко от _____ _____. И ещё один минус —
[хороший]   [супермаркет]

я живу далеко от _____ _____.
[университетский]   [бассейн]

Пока!
Джейсон

Имя и фамилия: _____   Число: _____

🔍 4.4 Упражнéние Ж. Что за дом?

Russian cultural institutions and headquarters of organizations often have names starting with the word "**дом**" followed by a genitive singular noun for the cultural area or profession in which the institution specializes. Read the institutional names below and decide what each institution promotes. If you are unfamiliar with the second word in some of the combinations, check it first in Google images (google.ru/images) to see if you can figure out the meaning. One has been done for you as an example.

Дом мýзыки	<u>House of Music</u>	Дом архитéктора	_____
Дом худóжника	_____	Дом актёра	_____
Дом кинó	_____	Дом культýры	_____
Дом журналúста	_____	Дом юрúста	_____
Дом мóды	_____	Дом йóги	_____

🔍 4.4 Упражнéние З. Как называ́ется э́та у́лица?

Street names in Russia are generally one of two types. Either there is an adjective before **у́лица** or **проспéкт** (e.g., **Пионéрская у́лица**, **Большóй проспéкт**) or the word **у́лица** is followed by a genitive "of" linkage (e.g., **у́лица Крáсного курсáнта**).

1. For this activity, use an online Russian map (maps.yandex.ru) for the city of Kazan'.

    The downtown area of Kazan' (a bit to the east of the Kremlyovskaya metro station) has both of these kinds of street names. On the map, find the Russian street names below and write them in the blanks.

    ___ Karl Marx Street = _____

    ___ Big Red Street = _____

    ___ University Street = _____

    ___ Pushkin Street = _____

    ___ Theatre Street = _____

    ___ Lev Tolstoy Street = _____

    ___ Gogol Street = _____

    ___ Kremlin Street = _____

2. When you are finished, go back and write the letter "G" next to street names that use the genitive "of" linkage.

Имя и фамилия: _____ Число: _____

4.4 Упражнéние И. More on Genitive "of" Linkage

It can often be difficult to see genitive "of" linkages when they are embedded in complete sentences. Read the sentences below, and underline the genitive phrase(s) in each one. Then give an English equivalent for the whole sentence.

1. Я дýмаю, что пéрвая бýква <u>этого слóва</u> — ш.
   _____

2. Ты знáешь áдрес <u>университéтской библиотéки</u>?
   _____

3. Я не пóмню фамúлию <u>твоегó дрýга</u>.
   _____

4. Тóни читáет пéрвую странúцу <u>интерéсного ромáна</u>.
   _____

5. На занятии мы смóтрим начáло <u>нóвого рýсского фúльма</u>.
   _____

6. Я не пóмню конéц <u>этого ромáна</u>.
   _____

7. Вы пóмните нóмер телефóна <u>нáшего преподавáтеля</u>?
   _____

8. Джош пóмнит, что дверь <u>нáшей квартúры</u> крáсная.
   _____

9. На ýлице вы вúдите машúну <u>вáшей хозяйки</u>?
   _____

Имя и фамилия: _____ Число: _____

4.4 Упражнение К. Новые глаголы

Complete this paragraph about Zoya Stepanovna and her neighbor by filling in the blanks with the present tense of the verbs provided.

Старая соседка Зои Степановны всегда всё _____ и _____. Она
  [видеть] [помнить]

_____, кто где _____, кто что _____, кто что
[знать] [жить] [делать]

_____ и кто когда _____. Соседка всегда _____: «Я всё
[смотреть] [отдыхать] [говорить]

_____ и всё _____, а ты, Зоя, ничего не _____ и не
[видеть] [помнить] [видеть]

_____». Зоя Степановна не _____, что соседи всё _____ и
[знать] [любить] [видеть]

_____.
[помнить]

4.4 Упражнёние Л. Sentence Completions

Complete each Russian sentence below with a logical conclusion. You will need to pay close attention to the pronouns, and remember that **понимать** (to understand) and **помнить** (to remember) are not the same verb. You can be creative, but stay within the bounds of the Russian that you know. Two possible completions for the first sentence have been provided as examples.

0. Я тебя люблю, потому что …

   ты очень добрый человек.   OR   ты меня так хорошо понимаешь.

1. Они его любят, но …

   _____

2. Вы меня понимаете, потому что …

   _____

3. Тони их знает, потому что …

   _____

4. Соседи её видят, но …

   _____

5. Мы вас не понимаем, потому что …

   _____

6. Преподаватель нас помнит, потому что …

   _____

Имя и фамилия: _____ Число: _____

4.5 Упражнéние А. Кафé «Идеáльная чáшка»

Below are sentences that summarize information in this episode, but the subject of each sentence is missing. Fill in the blanks with one of the four subjects listed in the word bank so that the sentences reflect what you have learned.

Амáнда	родители Амáнды	Жéня
	родители Жéни	

1. _____ ýчится на трéтьем кýрсе, а _____ ýчится в аспирантýре.
2. _____ ужé купúла чáйник и пьёт чай.
3. _____ говорúт, что в начáле ноябрá не óчень хóлодно.
4. _____ купúли дом в мáленьком гóроде недалекó от Сан-Францúско.
5. _____ óчень лю́бит рýсскую литератýру, хотя́ он изучáет математику.
6. _____ родилáсь в Сан-Францúско.
7. _____ учúлись в Калифорнúйском университéте в Бéркли.
8. _____ мáло знáет о рýсском искýсстве.
9. _____ дýмают, что учúться на филологúческом факультéте непрактúчно.
10. _____ ужé дýмает о рабóте, а _____ дýмает о диссертáции.
11. _____ учúлась в Стэ́нфордском университéте.

4.5 Упражнéние Б. Откýда онú пúшут?

a. In emails, Russians often start with a greeting from their current location. Match the greeting with the character who is most likely writing them.

____ 1. Привéт из Иркýтска! а. Амáнда
____ 2. Привéт из Казáни! б. Денúс
____ 3. Привéт из Калифóрнии! в. Джош
____ 4. Привéт из Москвы́! г. Кéйтлин
____ 5. Привéт из Нью-Йóрка! д. Преподавáтель Амáнды в США
____ 6. Привéт из Огáйо! е. Преподавáтель Джóша в США
____ 7. Привéт из Петербýрга! ж. Преподавáтель Кéйтлин в США
____ 8. Привéт из Техáса! з. Преподавáтель Тóни в США
____ 9. Привéт из Ярослáвля! и. Тóни

Имя и фамилия: _____ Число: _____

б. Keeping in mind that **из** requires the genitive case, write a similar greeting that you would use from your current:

city: _____

state: _____

country: _____

🎧 4.5 Упражнéние В. Откýда э́ти откры́тки (postcards)?

Some friends of Svetlana Borisovna are traveling around the European part of Russia. Listen to the six audio "postcards" they leave her as voicemail, and number the cities on the map in accordance with their travels.

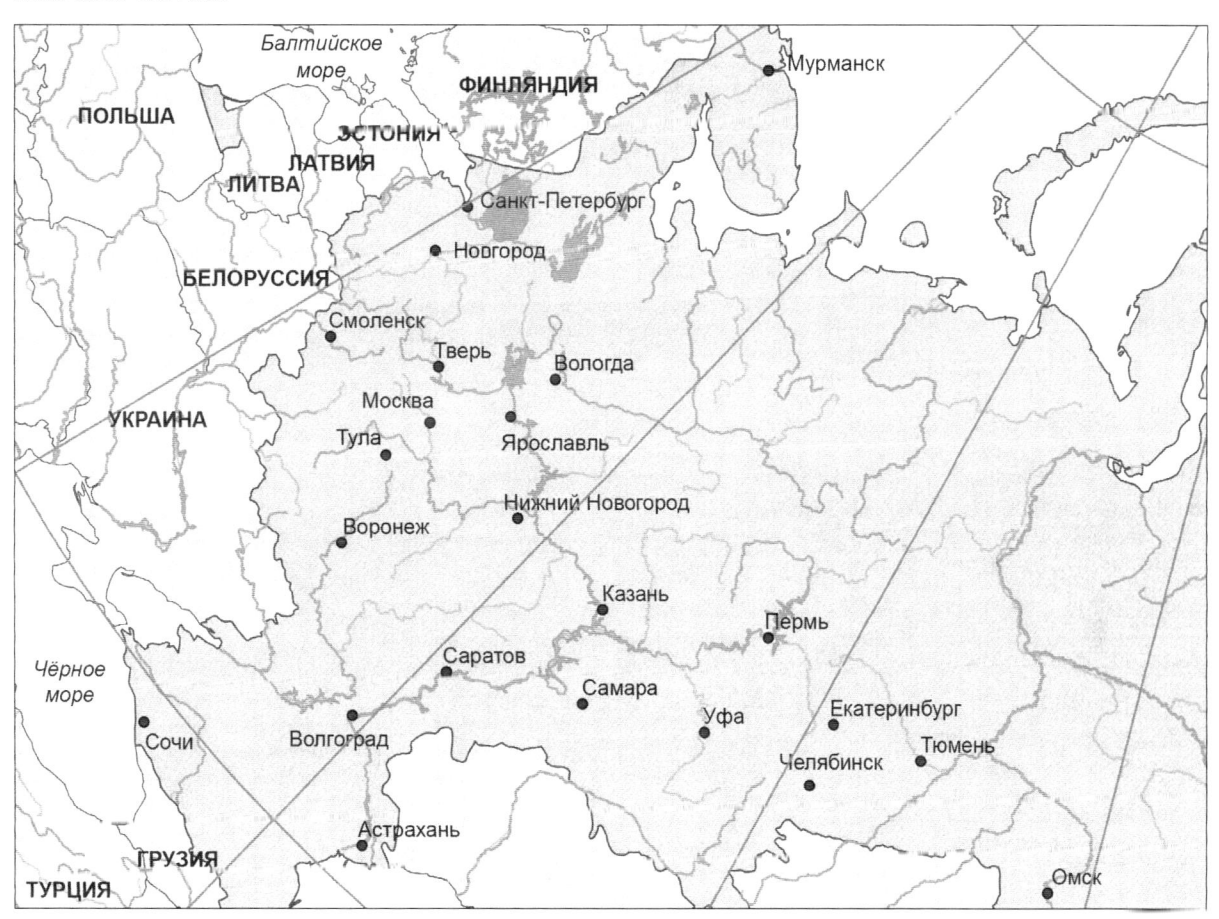

Между нами: Домáшние задáния — Урóк 4: часть 2

Имя и фамилия: _____ Число: _____

4.5 Упражнéние Г. Что вы вчерá дéлали?

Imagine that you are the person in each of the pictures below, responding to the question, "**Что вы вчерá дéлали?**" Your answers will all start with "**Вчерá я**...". Write your answers in complete sentences. Be sure to make correct gender agreements.

1.
2.
3.
4.
5.
6.

1. _____
2. _____
3. _____
4. _____
5. _____
6. _____

4.5 Упражнéние Д. Что ты дéлал(а) вчерá?

You want to know what your Russian friends Ira (*a female*) and Tolya (*a male*) were up to yesterday. Follow the directions below, modeling your questions after the example given. Vary your vocabulary, asking as many logical questions as you can.

a. Ask Ira and Tolya three yes/no questions each about their activities, starting each question with the person's name so they know whom you are addressing.

Образéц: Ира, ты вчерá игрáла на рояле?

1. _____
2. _____
3. _____
4. _____
5. _____
6. _____

Имя и фамилия: _____ Число: _____

б. Now, ask three questions directed to both of them at once (use the plural you, **вы**).

1. _____
2. _____
3. _____

4.5 Упражне́ние E. Немно́го о себе́ (A Bit About Myself)

Sveta has posted this short statement about her family. Fill in the blanks with the past tense forms of the indicated verbs.

Меня́ зову́т Све́та. Я живу́ в Ирку́тске, где я _____ [роди́ться]. Мой па́па _____ [роди́ться] в Перми́, но он _____ [учи́ться] в Новосиби́рске. Ма́ма _____ [роди́ться] в То́мске, но она́ то́же _____ [учи́ться] в Новосиби́рске. Ма́ма и па́па _____ [познако́миться], когда́ они́ вме́сте _____ [учи́ться] в университе́те на пе́рвом ку́рсе.

Имя и фамилия: _____   Число: _____

🎧 4.5 Упражнéние Ж. Немнóго о семьé

1. Robert is showing a picture of his family to his Russian friend Oleg. Fill in the missing information in this transcript of his comments.

   Олéг, смотри́, вот фотогрáфия нáшей семьи́. _____ _____

   зову́т Марк, а _____ _____ _____ зову́т Сáра. _____

   _____ _____ зову́т Майкл, а _____ _____

   зову́т Дэн. _____ _____ _____ зову́т Сáша.

2. Imagine that you are showing a picture of your family to a Russian friend. Tell him/her the name of each of your family members, using the model above as a guide.

   _____
   _____
   _____
   _____
   _____

4.5 Упражнéние З. Мáленькие словá

Match each Russian word to its English equivalent.

1. ____ Молодéц!   а. expensive
2. ____ мéжду прóчим   б. Let's do it.
3. ____ другóй   в. recently
4. ____ дóрого   г. Agreed!
5. ____ отли́чно   д. before, formerly
6. ____ Давáй.   е. by the way
7. ____ зáвтра   ж. then, later
8. ____ Договори́лись!   з. if
9. ____ мóжет быть   и. another
10. ____ рáньше   к. Good job!
11. ____ недáвно   л. It is time.
12. ____ я́сно   м. maybe
13. ____ éсли   н. It is clear.
14. ____ порá   о. tomorrow
15. ____ потóм   п. excellently

Имя и фамилия: _____   Число: _____

4.5 Упражнéние И. Кто когó знáет?

a. A Russian friend is asking you about the characters in our story. Your friend speaks quickly, so you repeat the question to yourself before answering. Fill in the blanks below to complete the missing endings on the names. All of them are direct objects, but remember that personal names for men are considered animate nouns. If no ending is required, write ø in the blank. An example has been done for you.

0. Натáлья Михáйловна знáет Амáнд_у_?

1. Амáнда знáет Зó____ Степáновн____?

2. Тóни знáет Олéг____ Пáнченко?

3. Жéня Кузнецóв знáет Кáт____ и Лéн____?

4. Кéйтлин знáет Тóни и Джóш____?

5. Денúс знáет Юри____ Николáевич____?

6. Натáлья Михáйловна знáет Марáт____ Азáтович____?

7. Амáнда, Джош, Кéйтлин и Тóни знáют Натáль____ Михáйловн____ Зáйцев____ и Денúс____ Гýрин____?

8. Амáнда знáет Жéн____ Кузнецóв____?

б. Answer the questions above based on what you know from our story. In your answers, replace both the subjects and the direct objects with pronouns. If you want to hedge on your answer, you can start your reply with **мóжет быть** (maybe).

0. Да, онá её знáет.
1. _____
2. _____
3. _____
4. _____
5. _____
6. _____
7. _____
8. _____

Мéжду нáми: Домáшние задáния   Урóк 4: часть 2   **171**

4.5 Упражне́ние К. Ситуа́ции

Review both episodes in Часть 2 and write out the Russian phrase that you would say in the following situations. Note that all of these prompts are connected.

1. You ask a stranger on the street, a middle-age woman, if she happens to know the name of the church in front of which you are standing.

2. The stranger does not remember, but asks you where you are from.

3. You answer that you are from America. You are studying at European University in Petersburg.

4. The stranger comments on how well you speak Russian.

5. The stranger asks if you like Russian literature. [*Use люби́ть.*]

6. You explain that you really like Pushkin and Bulgakov.

7. The stranger excuses herself and says that it is already five o'clock and [*she*] needs to go.

Имя и фамилия: _____   Число: _____

Урок 4: часть 3

4.6 Упражнéние А. Хочý рассказáть о Жéне

Pre-reading Activities and Skimming

1. After meeting Zhenya at **Идеáльная чáшка**, Amanda writes an email to her friends about him. Below is a list of topics that Amanda could possibly include in her email. Read the list, and in the left-hand column number the elements in the order that you think they would appear in the email

Predicted order		Actual order in text
_____	Zhenya and his studies	_____
_____	the neighborhood where she lives	_____
_____	how things are going in Petersburg	_____
_____	the room and the dorm where she lives	_____
_____	Zhenya's parents and family	_____
_____	greets her friend and asks how she is doing	_____
_____	about meeting Zhenya	_____

2. Now skim the episode and use the right-hand column to put the topics in the order that they are actually encountered in the text. Put an X on the line if a topic is not mentioned at all.

Checking Content in Detail

3. Make a list in English of four things in the story that happened **позавчерá** (the day before yesterday). Focus on phrases with the verbs **познакóмились**, **гуля́ли**, and **показáл**.

   а. _____
   б. _____
   в. _____
   г. _____

4. Why does Amanda want to buy a kettle? Write the exact Russian phrase from the text.

   _____

Мéжду нáми: Домáшние задáния   Урóк 4: часть 3   **173**

Имя и фамилия: _____ Число: _____

5. Amanda writes a number of things about Zhenya in this message. Copy down six phrases/sentences from the text that she uses to talk about him. If there are words that you do not know, look them up and put the English translation in parentheses above the word. One of the six phrases has already been written in for you. You will share your notes with others in class.

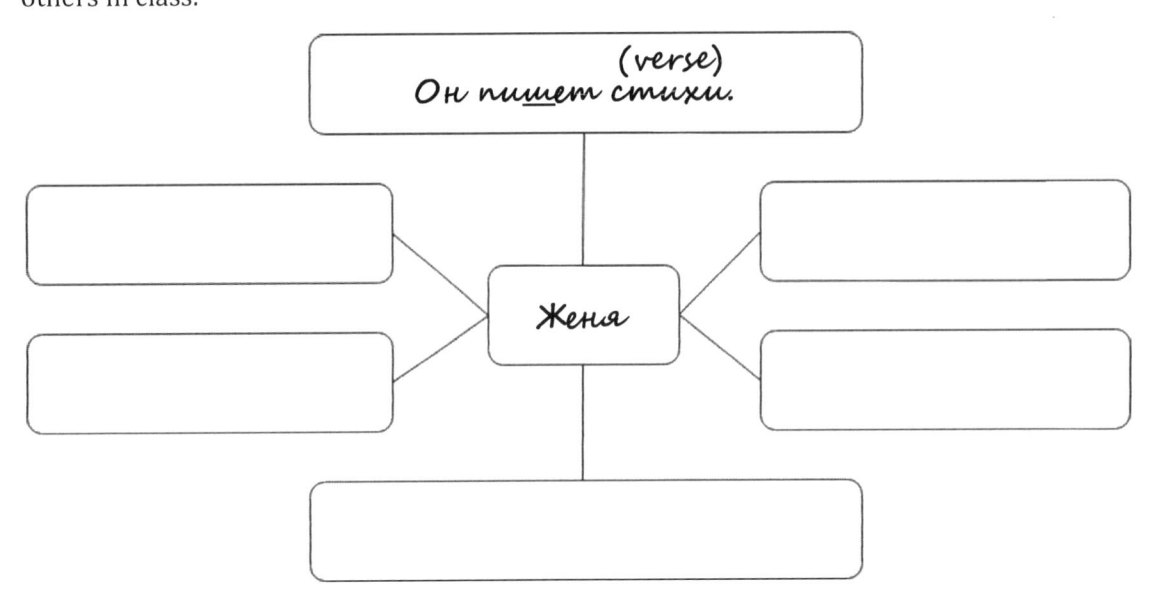

(verse)
Он пи*шет* стихи.

Женя

6. We learn some information about Zhenya's family in this episode. Copy down the relevant phrases from the text, putting them in the correct column.

Zhenya's father	Zhenya's mother	Zhenya's grandparents
•	•	•
•		•
•		

7. Although their conversation provided a lot of information, Amanda is still left with two unanswered questions about Zhenya and his family. Summarize these questions in English and then write out the exact phrases that Amanda uses in the text.

Summary in English	Russian phrases from the text

174   Урок 4: часть 3   *Между нами*: Домашние задания

Имя и фамилия: _____ Число: _____

8. In the final paragraph, Amanda mentions a misunderstanding that she often encounters in Petersburg. What is the problem, and how does she respond to it?

_____

_____

POST-READING ACTIVITIES

9. In many languages, words are often associated closely with other specific words (e.g., in English: bread and butter, singer and song, writer and novel). Match the words in the left-hand column with closely associated words in the right-hand column.

1. ____ стихи́
2. ____ спра́шивают
3. ____ юри́ст, матема́тик, фи́зик
4. ____ иску́сство
5. ____ иде́я
6. ____ ча́йник
7. ____ вчера́
8. ____ жизнь

а. отвеча́ют
б. чай
в. жить
г. худо́жник
д. ду́мать
е. поэ́т
ж. райо́н
з. профе́ссии
и. сего́дня

Между нами: Дома́шние зада́ния Уро́к 4: часть 3

Имя и фамилия: _____ Число: _____

10. When Amanda writes, "**Тогда́ э́то был** (was) **не Петербу́рг, тогда́ э́то был** (was) **Ленингра́д**," she is reflecting one of the many name changes that St. Petersburg has experienced since its founding in 1703.

- 1703-1914:   Санкт-Петербу́рг
- 1914-1924:   Петрогра́д
- 1924-1991:   Ленингра́д
- 1991-Present: Санкт-Петербу́рг and Петербу́рг (and Пи́тер, in informal speech)

In Soviet times there was a wide-spread joke about the three names and the kind of standard of living that they represented. The joke takes the form of an interview between a journalist and a very old man who was born in 1900. As you read the joke, select the answer that you think the old man gave to each question.

Журнали́ст берёт (is conducting) интервью́ у ста́рого мужчи́ны.

  Журнали́ст: Скажи́те, пожа́луйста, в како́м го́роде вы родили́сь?
  Ста́рый мужчи́на: а. В Санкт-Петербу́рге.
       б. В Ленингра́де

  Журнали́ст: А в како́м го́роде вы учи́лись?
  Ста́рый мужчи́на: а. В Петрогра́де.
       б. В Ленингра́де

  Журнали́ст: А в како́м го́роде вы сейча́с живёте?
  Ста́рый мужчи́на: а. В Санкт-Петербу́рге.
       б. В Петрогра́де
       в. В Ленингра́де

  Журнали́ст: А в како́м го́роде вы хоте́ли бы (would like to) жить?
  Ста́рый мужчи́на: а. В Санкт-Петербу́рге.
       б. В Петрогра́де
       в. В Ленингра́де

Имя и фамилия: _____   Число: _____

4.6 Упражнение Б. Квартира Тони в Техасе

Last year Tony shared an apartment with roommates, and now he is recalling the things that they had in that apartment. Fill in the blanks with the correct past-tense forms of **быть**. Remember to make your verbs agree with the things that *were*.

Это _____ очень недорогая квартира. Там у нас _____ большой балкон. Кухня и ванная _____ маленькие, но у нас _____ неплохие спальни. Моя комната _____ большая, но у меня _____ только одно очень маленькое окно.

4.6 Упражнение В. На первом курсе в Огайо

Caitlin is telling Rimma Yur'evna about her life as a college freshman. Complete her story by filling in the blanks with past-tense forms of the verbs provided in the word bank. You will need to use some verbs more than once. Note that the verbs in the word bank are all in the infinitive form.

быть (х3)	жить (х3)	родиться
разговаривать	пить	учиться
	познакомиться	

«Когда я _____ на первом курсе, я _____ в общежитии. У меня _____ небольшая комната.

В общежитии _____ студенты со всего мира (from the whole world). Например, на втором этаже _____ Томасо. Он очень интересный человек. Он из Перу. Он там _____.

Мы _____ в первый день семестра. Мы часто вместе _____ кофе в Старбаксе и _____ об американской культуре. Всё _____ очень интересно».

Между нами: Домашние задания   Урок 4: часть 3   177

Имя и фами́лия: _____ Число́: _____

4.6 Упражне́ние Г. У́тро в семье́ Ната́льи Миха́йловны

1. Complete this description of the breakfast habits of Natalya Mikhailovna and her family with appropriate present-tense forms of the verb **пить** [stem: **пьй–**].

У нас больша́я семья́, и у́тром (in the morning) мы почти́ не за́втракаем (eat breakfast), мы то́лько что́-нибудь (something) _____. Муж _____ чёрный ко́фе. Ба́бушка и де́душка всегда́ _____ то́лько горя́чий чай. Я _____ то́лько апельси́новый (orange) сок. А мла́дшая дочь На́дя всегда́ _____ горя́чее молоко́. А что вы _____ у́тром?

2. Answer Natalya Mikhailovna's question for yourself with a complete sentence.

_____

4.6 Упражне́ние Д. О ком? О чём?

Make complete present-tense sentences out of the words below so that they explain the topics about which our characters read, write, think, and talk. Consider whether you need to use **о** or **об**. If necessary, review the noun and adjective endings for the prepositional case before starting the exercise.

1. Ама́нда / чита́ть / о / ру́сский / иску́сство.

_____

2. То́ни / и / Джош / ду́мать / о / интере́сный / му́зыка.

_____

3. Ке́йтлин / писа́ть / сочине́ние / о / тата́рский / культу́ра.

_____

4. Мара́т Аза́тович / чита́ть / мно́го / о / спорт / и / би́знес.

_____

5. Светла́на Бори́совна / и / Со́ня / разгова́ривать / о / Джош.

_____

6. Дени́с / писа́ть / статья́ / о / исто́рия Росси́и.

_____

7. Ка́тя / и / Оле́г / ча́сто / разгова́ривать / о / жизнь.

_____

Имя и фамилия: _____   Число: _____

4.6 Упражнéние Е. А вы?

Complete the following sentences to say which topics interest you. If you are stuck for ideas, use the noun phrases from the word bank, which are all given in their dictionary forms. Remember to turn **о** into **об** before words starting with the vowels **а**, **и**, **о**, **у**, **э**.

моя́ семья́	ру́сская поли́тика	спорт
но́вая му́зыка	америка́нская исто́рия	университе́т
мой друг/моя́ подру́га	общежи́тие	но́вая литерату́ра
рабо́та	университе́тская баскетбо́льная кома́нда	телеви́дение

1. Я ча́сто разгова́риваю о _____.
2. Я люблю́ чита́ть о _____.
3. Я мно́го ду́маю о _____.
4. В э́том семе́стре я мно́го пишу́ о _____.
5. Я не люблю́ ду́мать о _____.

4.6 Упражнéние Ж. Pointing Things Out

Zhenya and his friend Masha are discussing a photo of Amanda that he took while they were at **Идеа́льная ча́шка**. Complete the conversation by choosing the correct form from those provided: either the unchanging **э́то** (it/this is a) or the modifier **э́тот** (this). You do not need to change any forms.

Образе́ц: [(Э́то) \ Э́тот] хоро́ший дом. [*This is a nice house.*]

Како́й? Вот [э́то \ (э́тот)] дом здесь? Нет! Он некраси́вый. [*This house.*]

Ма́ша: [Э́то \ Э́та] интере́сная фотогра́фия.

Же́ня: [Э́то \ Э́та] фотогра́фия? Почему́ ты так ду́маешь?

Ма́ша: Ну, Же́ня, скажи́, кто [э́то \ э́та] де́вушка на фотогра́фии?

Же́ня: [Э́то \ Э́та] одна́ аспира́нтка, кото́рая у́чится здесь в Петербу́рге.

Ма́ша. Интере́сно. А как зову́т [э́то \ э́ту] аспира́нтку?

Же́ня: Её зову́т Ама́нда.

Ма́ша: А фами́лия [э́то \ э́той] де́вушки?

Же́ня: Её фами́лия — Ли. Она́ из Аме́рики. Она́ здесь пи́шет диссерта́цию о ру́сском иску́сстве.

Ма́ша: [Э́то \ Э́ти] всё о́чень интере́сно.

Имя и фамилия: _____ Числó: _____

4.6 Упражнéние 3. Этот или другóй (This One or Another)?: Pointing Things Out

Complete the following dialogues with forms of the modifier **этот** (this one) or **другóй** (another, a different one) to clarify which object is being discussed.

1. — Кáтя óчень лю́бит _____ (this) магазин?

   — Нет, онá óчень лю́бит _____ (a different) магазин.

2. — Ты живёшь в _____ (this) общежитии?

   — Нет, я живу́ в _____ (a different) общежитии.

3. — Ты читáешь _____ (this) статью́?

   — Нет, я читáю _____ (a different) статью́.

4. — Ты живёшь на _____ (this) у́лице?

   — Нет, я живу́ на _____ (a different) у́лице.

5. — Ты смотрéл _____ (this) фильм?

   — Нет, я смотрéл _____ (a different) фильм.

4.6 Упражнéние И. Combining Sentences

a. Fill in the adjective endings for **котóрый** to make these sentences about characters from our story grammatically correct.

	вéрно / невéрно
1. Амáнда — студéнтка, котóр____ живёт в Петербу́рге в э́том году́.	____
2. Тóни — америкáнский студéнт, котóр____ у́чится в Ярослáвле в э́том году́.	____
3. Кéйтлин и Джош — студéнты, котóр____ сейчáс живу́т в Росси́и.	____
4. Светлáна Бори́совна — хозя́йка, котóр____ рабóтает в ресторáне.	____
5. Амáнда живёт в общежи́тии, котóр____ нахóдится недалекó от магази́на Эльдорáдо.	____
6. Ярослáвль — краси́вый гóрод, котóр____ нахóдится на рекé Вóлге.	____
7. Олéг не знáет студéнта, котóр____ показáл Амáнде магази́н Эльдорáдо.	____
8. Дени́с не знáет америкáнскую студéнтку, котóр____ у́чится в Казáни.	____

б. Now go back and read the sentences above and indicate whether they agree with what you know from the story line. Write **В** for **вéрно**, or **Н** for **невéрно** in the right-hand column.

Имя и фамилия: _____ Число: _____

4.6 Упражне́ние К. Ма́ленькие слова́
Match each Russian word to its English equivalent.

1. ____ вчера́
2. ____ где?
3. ____ како́й?
4. ____ кто?
5. ____ наде́юсь
6. ____ отку́да?
7. ____ позавчера́
8. ____ потому́ что
9. ____ почему́?
10. ____ ра́ньше
11. ____ хотя́
12. ____ чей?
13. ____ что?

а. although
б. because
в. before
г. day before yesterday
д. from where?
е. I hope
ж. what kind?; which one?
з. what?
и. where?
к. who?
л. whose?
м. why?
н. yesterday

Имя и фамилия: _____ Число: _____

🎧 4.6 Упражнéние Л. Вопрóсы, вопрóсы, вопрóсы

A Russian student who wants to interview you has left a voice message with questions for you to prepare. Listen to the message and write out the questions in Russian. Then write out your answers in complete sentences. Remember to put the new information at the end of your answer.

1. _____?
   Ваш отвéт: _____.
2. _____?
   Ваш отвéт: _____.
3. _____?
   Ваш отвéт: _____.
4. _____?
   Ваш отвéт: _____.
5. _____?
   Ваш отвéт: _____.
6. _____?
   Ваш отвéт: _____.
7. _____?
   Ваш отвéт: _____.
8. _____?
   Ваш отвéт: _____.
9. _____?
   Ваш отвéт: _____.
10. _____?
    Ваш отвéт: _____.

Имя и фамилия: _____   Число: _____

4.6 Упражнéние М. Интервью́

A celebrity from Russia is visiting your campus. You have an opportunity to interview him for your campus newspaper. You know that he works in the arts and has a spouse and two adult children. He does not speak English, so the interview needs to be in Russian.

Create a list of ten questions that you can ask to learn something about him and his family for your article. Remember that questions with question words (e.g., who, what, when, where, etc.) will yield more interesting answers than yes/no questions.

1. _____
2. _____
3. _____
4. _____
5. _____
6. _____
7. _____
8. _____
9. _____
10. _____

4.6 Упражнéние Н. Ситуáции

You are studying abroad in Russia and you want to tell your host mother about a new student in your group. How would you express the following thoughts?

1. I want to tell you a bit about a new student.

   _____

2. The new student is named ___ [*your choice*].

   _____

3. We became acquainted the day before yesterday.

   _____
   _____

4. The new student was born in Irkutsk, but is now is studying in Petersburg.

   _____
   _____

5. Yesterday we strolled and chatted about life in Petersburg.

   _____
   _____

Имя и фамилия: _____   Число: _____

IMAGE INFORMATION

4.4 Упражне́ние Б. Что э́то тако́е?
1. "Apothecary symbol" is in the public domain. Last accessed October 28, 2015. http://www.clipartbest.com/clipart-9TRo4LeTe
2. "Russian Orthodox Church" by Freepik is licensed under CC BY 3.0. Last accessed October 28, 2015. http://www.flaticon.com/free-icon/russian-orthodox-church_75047
3. "Hot coffee rounded cup on a plate…" by Freepik is licensed under CC BY 3.0. Last accessed October 28, 2015. http://www.flaticon.com/free-icon/hot-coffee-rounded-cup-on-a-plate-from-side-view_37908
4. "Film Roll" by Freepik is licensed under CC BY 3.0. Last accessed October 28, 2015. http://www.flaticon.com/free-icon/film-roll_61342
5. "Swimmer" by Freepik is licensed under CC BY 3.0. Last accessed October 28, 2015. http://www.flaticon.com/free-icon/swimmer_47743
6. "Closed Mail Envelope" by Pavel Kozlov in licensed under CC BY 3.0. Last accessed October 28, 2015. http://www.flaticon.com/free-icon/closed-mail-envelope_70148
7. "Fork and knife in cross" by Freepik is licensed under CC BY 3.0. Last accessed October 28, 2015. http://www.flaticon.com/free-icon/fork-and-knife-in-cross_45552
8. "Stadium" by Freepik is licensed under CC BY 3.0. Last accessed October 28, 2015. http://www.flaticon.com/free-icon/stadium_53213
9. "Antique elegant building with columns" by Freepik is licensed under CC BY 3.0. Last accessed October 28, 2015. http://www.flaticon.com/free-icon/antique-elegant-building-with-columns_28620

4.5 Упражне́ние В. Отку́да э́ти откры́тки (postcards)?
Map created by Di Shi, Director of Cartographic Services Lab, University of Kansas. Released under a CC BY license.

Имя и фамилия: _____   Число: _____

Урок 5: часть 1

5.1 Упражнение А. Дни недели

You are discussing plans with a Russian visitor, and he is confused about dates and days. Use the calendar below to tell him on which day of the week the dates he asks about occur. The first one has been done for you.

октябрь						
пн	вт	ср	чт	пт	сб	вс
			1	2	3	4
5	6	7	8	9	10	11
12	13	14	15	16	17	18
19	20	21	22	23	24	25
26	27	28	29	30	31	

0. А какой день восьмое?   <u>Восьмое — четверг</u>_____.
1. А какой день пятое?   _____.
2. А какой день второе?   _____.
3. А какой день четвёртое?   _____.
4. А какой день десятое?   _____.
5. А какой день седьмое?   _____.
6. А какой день тринадцатое? _____.

5.1 Упражнение Б. Месяцы

Unscramble the letters below to spell out the name of the months in Russian. Then number them in the order in which they occur on the calendar.

____ льюи   ____ борьян   ____ йам

____ арельфв   ____ трам   ____ тябокрь

____ ньястреб   ____ юньи   ____ стугав

____ пларье   ____ бекрадь   ____ рьянав

Между нами: Домашние задания   Урок 5: часть 1   185

Имя и фамилия: _____ Число: _____

🎧 5.1 Упражнéние В. В какóй день?

You put your activities for this week on sticky notes, but cannot remember on which day the events will happen. Fortunately, your friend remembers all of the events and when they are scheduled. Listen and write in the day on which each event will take place using the preposition **в** and the day of the week in the accusative case. The first one has been done for you.

- спать весь день
- днём работа
- фильм «Стиляги»
- ужин в кафе «Пицца Хат» в 6 часов
- контрольная работа
- встреча Русского клуба — **в понедельник**
- сочинение на тему «Международная политика России сегодня»

Имя и фамилия: _____ Число: _____

5.1 Упражнéние Г. Где вы бы́ли?

Think about your schedule for the past week and where you were at certain times. Using at least one element from each column, create six sentences that accurately reflect your recent activities. An example sentence has been provided.

Remember that to say "on a day of a week," use **в** with the accusative case form of the day; to give location, use **в** or **на** with the prepositional case form of the noun.

| в | понедéльник
вто́рник
среда́
четвéрг
пя́тница
суббо́та
воскресéнье | у́тром
днём
вéчером
но́чью | я | быть | в
на | рабо́та
рестора́н
университéт
лéкция
библиотéка
фи́тнес-це́нтр
общежи́тие
концéрт
центр
?? |

0. <u>В срéду вéчером я был(á) на лéкции.</u>
1. _____ .
2. _____ .
3. _____ .
4. _____ .
5. _____ .
6. _____ .

🎧 5.2 Упражнéние А. Как живу́т на́ши сосéдки

Listen to this description of the daily activities of two students. Then number the activities below in the order in which the students do them. Before listening, look up any words that you do not know.

____ встаю́т   ____ ложа́тся спать

____ гото́вят дома́шние зада́ния   ____ гото́вят у́жин

____ за́втракают   ____ одева́ются

____ éдут в университéт   ____ éдут домо́й

____ смо́трят телеви́зор   ____ отдыха́ют

____ обéдают в столо́вой   ____ чи́стят зу́бы

____ иду́т в библиотéку

Мéжду нáми: Домáшние задáния Уро́к 5: часть 1 **187**

Имя и фамилия: _____ Число: _____

5.2 Упражнение Б. Что я делаю каждый день?
Imagine that you are Caitlin and label the pictures below using the first-person singular form of the needed verb.

Я _____

Я _____

Я _____

Я _____

Я _____

Вечером я _____

Я _____
_____

Я _____
_____

Я _____

5.2 Упражнение В. А вы?
What are your daily routines? Finish each sentence with at least four activities that you do at each time of day. List the actions in the order that you do them.

1. Утром я …
   _____
   _____

2. Днём я …
   _____
   _____

3. Вечером я …
   _____
   _____

Имя и фамилия: _____ Число: _____

5.2 Упражнéние Г. Нóвый сосéд / Нóвая сосéдка по кварти́ре

You are looking for a new roommate to share an apartment. What questions would you ask a prospective roommate about his/her daily routine? You can use question words (e.g., **Где?** **Когдá?**) as well as questions about frequency (e.g., **чáсто**, **обы́чно**, **кáждый день**). Since the prospective roommates are all close to you in age, use **ты** in your questions. Come up with ten questions that make use of a variety of vocabulary.

1. _____
2. _____
3. _____
4. _____
5. _____
6. _____
7. _____
8. _____
9. _____
10. _____

5.2 Упражнéние Д. Хорóший сосéд / хорóшая сосéдка

Write five sentences describing the habits of a good roommate. One has been done for you as an example.

0. По-мóему, хорóший сосéд по кварти́ре ложи́тся спать не óчень пóздно.
1. _____
2. _____
3. _____
4. _____
5. _____

Имя и фамилия: _____ Число: _____

5.2 Упражнéние Е. Ужáсные сосéди

Imagine that you have really horrible roommates. Complete each of the sentences below with one or two phrases that detail their objectionable behavior. Remember to make the verbs agree with their subjects, but to use an infinitive if the main verb is a conjugated form of **любить**.

У меня ужáсные сосéди по квартире. Их зовýт _____ и _____.

Они рéдко ____ __ _____ _____.

Они никогдá не _____.

Они всё врéмя _____.

Они лю́бят _____ и _____, когдá я сплю.

5.2 Упражнéние Ж. Кудá вы идёте?

Fill in the blanks with the appropriate form of the verb **идти**.

Абдýловы сегóдня _____ на интерéсный концéрт.

Марáт Азáтович ждёт (is waiting) и смóтрит в окнó (out the window). Он видит, как сосéд

Анатóлий Петрóвич _____ по ýлице. Он смóтрит на часы́. Ужé шесть часóв!

Марáт Азáтович спрáшивает: «Ри́мма, где ты? Ты _____? Мы ужé

опáздываем.»

Ри́мма Ю́рьевна отвечáет: «Я сейчáс _____.»

На ýлице Анатóлий Петрóвич видит их и спрáшивает: «Ри́мма Ю́рьевна и Марáт

Азáтович, кудá вы _____?»

Ри́мма Ю́рьевна отвечáет: «Мы _____ в теáтр.»

5.2 Упражнéние З. Кудá вы éдете?

The characters below have run into each other in the metro and are talking about where people are going. Since it is clear from the context that they are all going by some form of transportation, fill in the blanks with the appropriate form of **éхать**.

В метрó

И́ра: Привéт, Амáнда! Привéт, Жéня! Кудá вы _____?

Амáнда: Я _____ на Нéвский проспéкт, а Жéня _____ в библиотéку

Технологи́ческого институ́та.

И́ра: Понятно. А вон там Мáша и Лéна. Они _____ на вокзáл (train

station), а потóм в Цáрское селó. Они хотя́т погуля́ть там в пáрке.

Амáнда: А мы _____ тудá зáвтра.

Имя и фамилия: _____ Число: _____

5.3 Упражне́ние А. Име́йл Ке́йтлин

Pre-Reading Activities: Skimming

а. The words «Пишу́ из Каза́ни» begin the first of the six main paragraphs of Caitlin's email. Each paragraph addresses a different topic. Read the list of topics below and then skim the email to locate where Caitlin discusses each of them. Place a number 1-6 in each blank to indicate the paragraph in which the topic is discussed.

_____ details about her conversation practice teacher Mila

_____ parts of the city that Caitlin has learned about in the first month

_____ how she spends evenings and weekends

_____ some comments about the Abdulov family

_____ information about the lecture courses Caitlin is taking

_____ details about her phonetics and grammar classes

Checking Content in Detail

б. Caitlin is taking five courses this semester. Look through her email and find the names of the courses, noting the days of the week when she has them. Complete the table with Russian words and phrases from the text, using time expressions that include prepositions. The first one has been done for you.

ку́рсы	в како́й день? / в каки́е дни?
0. фоне́тика	в понеде́льник, в четве́рг
1.	
2.	
3.	
4.	

в. Caitlin gives short descriptions of three of her teachers. Write down the name of each teacher, and two or three Russian phrases from the text that she uses to describe them. Give the English equivalent of each phrase in the third column.

преподава́тель	фра́зы из те́кста	англи́йский эквивале́нт
	• • •	
	• • •	

Между нами: Дома́шние зада́ния   Уро́к 5: часть 1   191

Имя и фамилия: _____   Число: _____

преподаватель	фразы из текста	английский эквивалент
	• • •	

г. Write down in English two or three points about what Caitlin does differently on the weekends.

1. _____
2. _____
3. _____

д. Caitlin's email is a good model of how to write a friendly message to someone with whom you are on formal terms. How does Caitlin express the following phrases in Russian?

Dear [first name and patronymic]: _____

Yours,: _____

Write (soon): _____

I hope that everything is okay with you.: _____

Two of the phrases used above are marked for gender in Russian. Place an asterisk (*) next to the phrase that is dependent on the gender of the person who is writing; place two asterisks (**) next to the phrase that is dependent on the gender of the person who will receive the message.

🔍 POST-READING ACTIVITY

е. О культуре: To get a sense of how well-known the phrase **великий и могучий русский язык** is, search for it at google.ru. Make sure to put it in English quotation marks to search for the exact phrase. You will need to use a laptop or desktop for this activity as most mobile devices do not provide the total number of results found during a search.

I found _____ [*write in number*] results.

The 19th-century writer Ivan Sergeevich Turgenev was the first to pen the phrase **великий, могучий русский язык** (without the conjunction **и**) in an essay about language, nation, and national destiny. Today, the phrase has a life of its own. Caitlin's teacher is possibly using it with some irony as he struggles to explain the nuances of Russian grammar in response to students' questions.

Имя и фамилия: _____ Число: _____

5.3 Упражнéние Б. Что вы хоти́те?

Using the cues provided, create sentences indicating the item that each person wants. Remember that you will need to conjugate the verb **хотéть** to match the subject pronoun and that the items will need to be in the accusative case because they function as direct objects.

1. Я _____ _____.   2. Она́ _____ _____.

3. Ты _____ _____.   4. Вы _____ _____.

5.3 Упражнéние В. Пла́ны

Complete the following mini-dialogues with the appropriate forms of **хотéть**.

<u>В гости́нице разгова́ривают тури́сты.</u>

— Мы _____ за́втракать.

— А что вы _____ де́лать?

<u>В рестора́не.</u>

Официа́нт: Что вы бу́дете пить?

Клие́нт: Я _____ чай, а мои́ друзья́, наве́рное, _____ кóфе.

<u>В общежи́тии разгова́ривают студе́нты.</u>

Ма́ша: Ва́ля, ты _____ занима́ться в библиотéке?

Ва́ля: Нет. Мóжет быть, Ди́ма _____ там занима́ться.

Имя и фамилия: _____   Число: _____

5.3 Упражнение Г. Джош в октябре

In September Josh had some difficulty adjusting to his new life in Irkutsk. He had trouble getting up on time, was late getting to classes, and was spending a lot of money eating out. By October, however, he had settled into a new routine that is described below. Read the paragraph and fill in each blank with an appropriate present-tense form of a verb from the word bank. There are two extra verbs, and no verb is used more than once.

Завтракать	ложиться	Принимать
Ужинать	писать	Идти
Помнить	смотреть	Слушать
Опаздывать	спать	Обедать
Хотеть	чистить	Вставать
	готовить	

Уже октябрь, и у Джоша теперь всё в порядке. Утром он _____ рано, потому что он купил хороший будильник. Он _____ душ, одевается и _____ зубы. Он не только пьёт кофе, но и _____. Джош теперь никогда не _____ в университет.

Днём он _____ в столовой, потому что там не так дорого, как в кафе. В шесть часов (o'clock) он говорит друзьям: «Пока!» и _____ домой. Там Светлана Борисовна _____ ужин, и они вместе _____.

Вечером Джош _____ имейлы и делает домашние задания. Он ещё немного _____ музыку или _____ телевизор, но не так много, как раньше. И он _____ спать не очень поздно, и _____ семь часов. Утром не трудно вставать.

Имя и фамилия: _____ Число: _____

5.3 Упражнéние Д. Ситуáции

A friend of yours studies sociology and is curious to learn about how Russian university students organize their time. Help her to translate her survey questions into Russian. Since the questions are addressed to adult strangers, you will use **вы**.

1. When do you usually get up in the morning?

   _____

2. When do you usually go to bed?

   _____

3. Do you usually eat breakfast?

   _____

4. Do you usually eat lunch in the cafeteria?

   _____

5. Where do you usually study?

   _____

6. Where do you usually eat supper?

   _____

7. Do you usually take a shower in the morning or in the evening?

   _____

Имя и фамилия: _____ Число: _____

Уро́к 5: часть 2

5.4 Упражне́ние А. Ско́лько сейча́с вре́мени?
Write out the times shown below as words. Pay attention to the form of **час** needed.

1. _____
   _____

2. _____
   _____

3. _____
   _____

4. _____
   _____

5. _____
   _____

6. _____
   _____

7. _____
   _____

8. _____
   _____

5.4 Упражне́ние Б. Временны́е пояса́ (Time Zones)
Using the information provided in this episode, complete the sentences below with the appropriate times. Use the 24-hour clock.

1. Éсли сейча́с в Ирку́тске пять часо́в, то в Москве́ _____.
2. Éсли сейча́с на Камча́тке два́дцать три часа́, то в Москве́ _____.
3. Éсли сейча́с на Камча́тке двена́дцать часо́в, то в Москве́ _____.
4. Éсли сейча́с во Владивосто́ке четы́ре часа́, то в Ирку́тске _____.
5. Éсли сейча́с в Новосиби́рске пять часо́в, то в Каза́ни _____.
6. Éсли сейча́с в Екатеринбу́рге во́семь часо́в, то в Петербу́рге _____.

Между нами: Дома́шние зада́ния

Имя и фамилия: _____   Число: _____

5.5 Упражнéние А. Мобильная жизнь

a. Fill in the subject of each sentence below to accurately reflect the events of the episode.

1. _____ сегóдня éдет на экскýрсию.
2. _____ спрáшивает, éдет Кéйти в Москвý или нет.
3. _____ отвечáет, что Кремль есть и в Казáни.
4. _____ не знáет, что в Казáни есть Кремль.
5. _____ говорит, что в егó гóроде тóже есть Кремль.
6. _____ спрáшивает, скóлько сейчáс врéмени в Иркýтске.
7. _____ сегóдня идёт на концéрт грýппы Би-2.
8. _____ завидует, что Джош идёт на такóй интерéсный концéрт.

б. In the contexts given below, what do the verb choices that Caitlin makes tell us about how she is getting to her destination? Provide your answers in English using the column on the far right.

Context	Statement	Implication
1. *In the first dialog with Amanda, she says:*	Я éду в центр.	_____
2. *In the second dialog with Tony, she says:*	Мы идём в Кремль.	_____

в. The word **кремль** in Old Russian was the name of a fortified city center. Place a check mark next to the cities that have a **кремль** according to the episode.

___ Москвá   ___ Петербýрг   ___ Казáнь   ___ Ярослáвль   ___ Иркýтск

г. Which of the words below can close an informal conversation?

___ покá   ___ здóрово   ___ красиво   ___ счастливо

🎧 5.5 Упражнéние Б. Уикéнд Гáли

As Galya tells you about her weekend, you will not necessarily recognize all of the words that she uses. You should, however, be able to hear whether she refers to places as locations (by listening for the prepositional case ending) or as destinations (by listening for the accusative case ending). Place a check mark in the appropriate column.

	1	2	3	4	5	6	7
Где? Location							
Кудá? Destination							

Имя и фамилия: _____ Число: _____

5.5 Упражне́ние В. Биле́ты (Tickets)

The sentences below include information on people who have bought **биле́ты** for a train. Since word order is flexible in Russian, you will need to look at the grammatical endings to determine whether the city is the location where the person bought the ticket (in the prepositional case) or the destination to which the person will travel (in the accusative case).

Read the sentences and then draw an arrow on the map from the city where the person bought their ticket to their final destination. Label the arrow with the number of the sentence. The first one has been done for you.

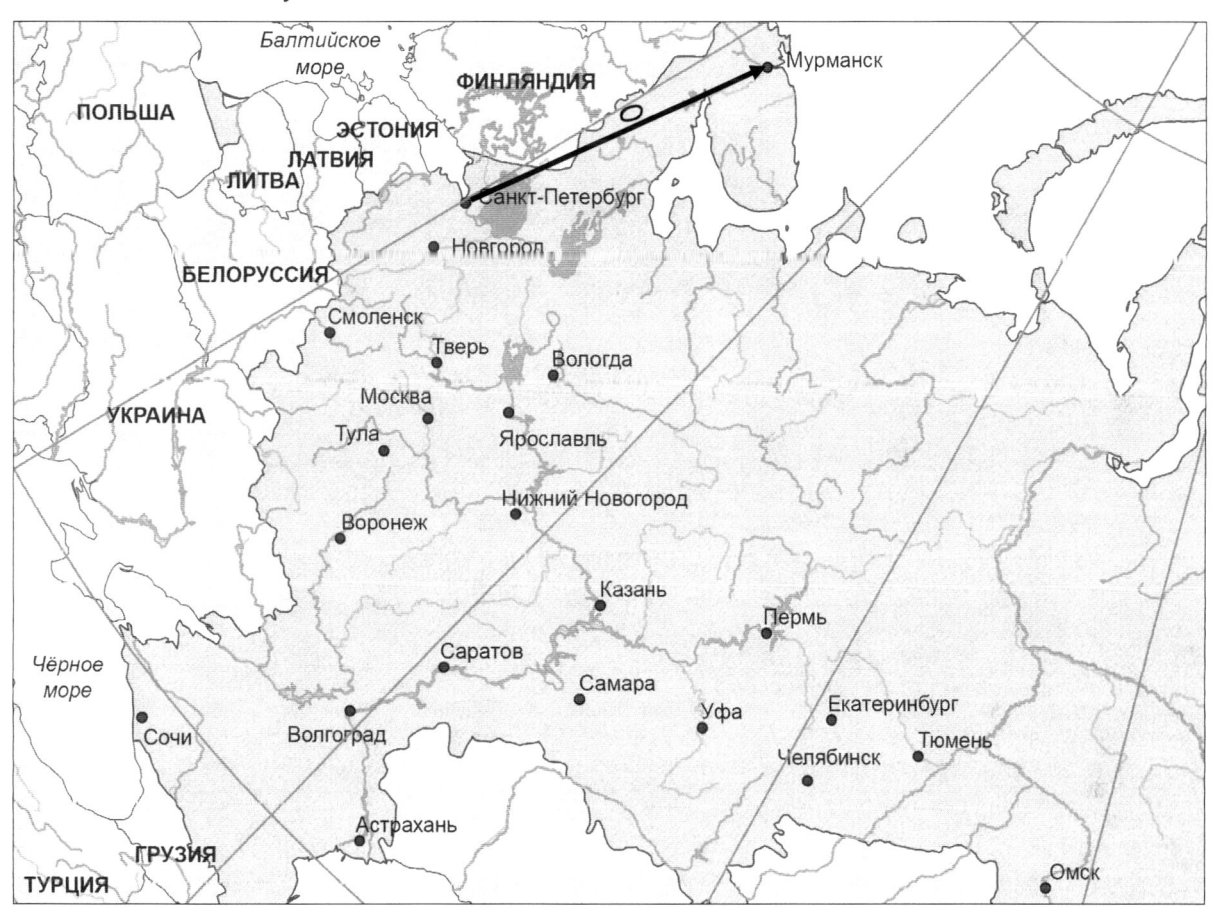

0. В Петербу́рге Серге́й купи́л биле́т в Му́рманск.
1. Ни́на купи́ла в Ту́ле биле́т в Москву́.
2. В Уфу́ Андре́й купи́л биле́т в Сара́тове.
3. В Москве́ А́ня купи́ла биле́т в Ни́жий Но́вгород.
4. То́ля купи́л биле́т в Воро́неж в Волгогра́де.
5. В Смоле́нск Ма́ша купи́ла биле́т в Каза́ни.
6. В Но́вгороде Ю́рий Никола́евич купи́л биле́т в Тверь.

Имя и фамилия: _____   Число: _____

5.5 Упражнéние Г. Что дéлают на э́той карти́нке?

Fill in the blanks below to caption the pictures. If the picture shows motion (indicated by an arrow), you will need to use a form of **идти́** or **éхать** and to put the noun in the accusative case to show destination. If the picture shows location, you will need to put ø in the blank for the verb and to put the noun in the prepositional case to show location.

1. Дéти _____ в парк___.

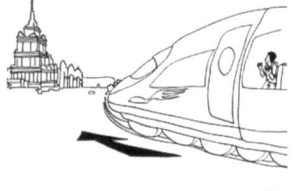

2. Тури́ст _____ в Москв___.

3. Студéнтка _____ в консерватóри___.

4. Преподавáтель _____ в аудитóри___.

5. Молодóй человéк _____ на заня́ти___.

6. Молодóй человéк и дéвушка _____ в парк___.

7. Дéти _____ в шкóл___.

8. Тури́ст _____ в Москв___.

9. Дéти _____ в клáсс___.

10. Мáльчик _____ в кафé.

Имя и фамилия: _____   Число: _____

5.5 Упражнéние Д. Плáны

Think about your schedule and those of your friends for the next seven days. Use a word (or phrase) from each of the columns below to create ten truthful statements about where you all will be going.

If you are going out of town, you will need to use the verb **éхать**. If you are going to places within town, you will need to use **идти́**. Where you see "??" in a column, you may add your own words.

в	понедéльник втóрник средá четвéрг пя́тница суббóта воскресéнье	у́тром днём вéчером нóчью	я мой сосéд мой друг моя́ подрýга мои́ друзья́ ??	идти́ éхать	в на	Рабóта кафé магази́н университéт заня́тия библиотéка столóвая парк теáтр кинó цéрковь Бóстон Чикáго Сан-Франци́ско ??

1. _____.
2. _____.
3. _____.
4. _____.
5. _____.
6. _____.
7. _____.
8. _____.
9. _____.
10. _____.

Имя и фамилия: _____ Число: _____

5.5 Упражнéние E. New Verbs in -ова-ть

Complete each of the following sentences with an appropriate form of **фотографи́ровать** or **целова́ть** in the present tense. Then indicate the picture that best illustrates the sentence.

	Кака́я картинка?

1. На экску́рсии в Каза́нском кремле́ мы _____ Спа́сскую ба́шню. ____

2. Я _____ му́жа. ____

3. Други́е студе́нты в на́шей гру́ппе _____ стари́нную ба́шню Сюю́мбике́. ____

4. Мара́т Аза́тович _____ жену́. ____

5. Гид спра́шивает, почему́ вы не _____ э́ту це́рковь? ____

6. — Кéйтлин, я не понима́ю, почему́ ты _____ э́ти ста́рые деревя́нные (wooden) дома́. Ведь в Каза́ни есть краси́вые но́вые зда́ния!

   — Я их _____ , потому́ что они́ о́чень необы́чные. ____

7. Дéвушки здесь _____ ма́льчика. ____

8. Ро́берт _____ «Голубу́ю мече́ть». ____

9. Мы _____ дéвушку. ____

10. Ама́нда _____ Жéню. ____

а. б. в. г. д.

е. ж. з. и. к.

Имя и фамилия: _____   Число: _____

5.5 Упражнéние Ж. The Power of Suffixes: Vocabulary Building

The suffix **-овать** is widely used in Russian, where it can be added to a foreign word to make a new verb. See if you can recognize these "Russian" verbs.

по-рýсски	по-англи́йски
1. паркова́ть	_____
2. аплоди́ровать	_____
3. экспорти́ровать	_____
4. анализи́ровать	_____
5. гаранти́ровать	_____
6. демонстри́ровать	_____
7. танцева́ть	_____
8. контроли́ровать	_____
9. регули́ровать	_____
10. рекомендова́ть	_____
11. флиртова́ть	_____

5.5 Упражнéние З. Пла́ны: Ты мо́жешь …?

Complete the following dialogues with the appropriate form of the verb **мочь**.

1. *Звоно́к (The phone rings).*

    Тóни говори́т: Алло́!

    Кéйтлин говори́т: Тóни, приве́т! Ты _____ говори́ть сейча́с?

    Тóни отвеча́ет: Приве́т, Кéйти. К сожале́нию, сейча́с я не _____.

    Я иду́ на встре́чу (meeting). Мы _____ поговори́ть

    (to chat) ве́чером?

    Кéйтлин: Хорошо́.

2. Джош спра́шивает: Ребя́та, вы _____ занима́ться сего́дня ве́чером?

    У нас ведь контро́льная рабо́та ско́ро.

    Ни́на отвеча́ет: Я _____ сего́дня ве́чером, а Анто́н не

    _____. А други́е студе́нты в на́шей гру́ппе

    то́лько за́втра ве́чером.

Имя и фамилия: _____ Число: _____

5.5 Упражнéние И. Вот какие у нас правила!

Your task is to make a set of rules for one of the locations listed below. Place a check mark next to the location you choose.

_____ Это правила театра. _____ Это правила библиотеки.

_____ Это правила общежития. _____ Это правила музея.

Now come up with at least three actions that are allowed (**мóжно**) and three that are prohibited (**нельзя́**) in that location. For example:

У нас в общежитии нельзя́ курить. (In our dormitory one may not smoke.)

You can use different times of the day and days of the week to give nuance to your rules. If you need some ideas about what actions you might allow or prohibit, consult the word bank below.

play an instrument	play soccer	drink coffee
talk loudly at night	sleep	eat supper
Study	listen to music	read text messages
Smoke	take pictures	applaud
Dance	flirt	eat breakfast

1. У нас в _____ мóжно _____.

   мóжно _____.

   мóжно _____.

2. У нас в _____ нельзя́ _____.

   нельзя́ _____.

   нельзя́ _____.

5.6 Упражнéние А. Денис éдет в Ярославль

Find and correct the eight factual mistakes in the following summary. There may be more than one way to correct a mistake, but make sure that your correction fits the grammatical context.

Денис éдет в Ярославль в суббóту. Он éдет туда на пóезде, потому́ что это недорого. Он будет у Зóи Степановны три дня. В пятницу вéчером Тóни будет дóма. Зóя Степановна говорит, что это не проблéма, и что завтрак ужé готóв.

Аманда думала éхать в Ярославль в суббóту, потому́ что там открывается нóвая выставка русского искусства. Денис говорит, что не надо идти в пéрвый день работы выставки, потому́ что там будет мáло народу. Аманда понимает, что Денис, наверное, рад.

204 урок 5: часть 2 *между нами:* Домашние задания

🎧 5.6 Упражнéние Б. Когдá начинáется ... ? (When Does ... Start?)

1. Caitlin is trying to figure out what cultural activities to attend this week. Listen to her options and write in the starting time for the events.

   The times you hear will be in **официáльный стиль** (24-hour clock format). Write out the numbers as words along with the preposition **в** and the appropriate form of **час**. Then, in the column on the right, write out the time in digits using the 12-hour clock (a.m. and p.m.). The first one has been done for you as an example.

		12-hour clock
0.	Концéрт классúческой мýзыки начинáется __в девятнáдцать часóв__ .	7 p.m.
1.	Лéкция о рýсском искýсстве начинáется _____ .	_____
2.	Экскýрсия в Кремль начинáется _____ .	_____
3.	Фильм «Брат» начинáется _____ .	_____
4.	Нóвости (the news) начинáются _____ .	_____
5.	В суббóту óпера «Евгéний Онéгин» начинáется _____ .	_____
6.	Выставка в Истори́ческом музéе открывáется _____ .	_____

2. If you were Caitlin, which activity would you most want to do, and why? You may answer in English.

Имя и фамилия: _____   Число: _____

5.6 Упражнéние B. Short-Form Adjectives

Fill in each blank with an appropriate word from the word bank. Note that there are two extra words.

Прав	готóва	свобóдна
Свобóден	рáды	занятá
Готóв	правá	зáняты
	рáда	

1. У Андрéя все заня́тия в понедéльник, срéду и пя́тницу. Знáчит, во втóрник и четвéрг он _____.

2. В суббóту Гáля _____ весь день — у неё рабóта в магази́не. Рабóта начинáется в 7.00 часóв утрá, и онá идёт домóй тóлько в 9.00 часóв вéчера.

3. Мáма пи́шет в имéйле, что онá _____, что у меня́ всё в поря́дке.

4. Амáнда тепéрь знáет, что Кáтя _____. В магази́не Эльдорáдо мóжно купи́ть всё, что ну́жно.

5. Жéня говори́т, что на фотогрáфии — Нéвский проспéкт. Но он не _____, э́то ведь не Нéвский проспéкт, а Литéйный проспéкт.

6. Марáт, где ты? Зáвтрак ужé _____, а ты ещё одевáешься.

7. Мы óчень _____, что ещё есть билéты на концéрт.

8. К сожалéнию, кварти́ра не _____. Там ещё дéлают ремóнт.

| Имя и фамилия: _____ | Число: _____ |

5.6 Упражнение Г. Диалоги

Fill in the blanks with the appropriate form of the words cued in English. Remember that with **я**, the short-form adjective will agree with the gender of the person speaking. With **ты**, the short-form adjective will agree with the gender of the person being addressed, while with **вы**, the short-form adjective will always be plural.

1. — Римма Юрьевна, вы _____ ?
   [ready]

   — Да, я уже _____ .
   [ready]

2. — Зоя, ты _____ сегодня вечером?
   [free]

   — Нет, я _____ .
   [busy]

3. — Антон, ты _____ .
   [right]

   — Конечно, я _____ . Эти музыканты отлично играют.
   [right]

4. — Лена, ты _____ , что слушала концерт вчера?
   [glad]

   — Конечно, я _____ .
   [glad]

5.6 Упражнение Д. Зоя Степановна говорит по телефону

a. Complete the dialog below using forms of the verb **быть** in the future tense.

— Алло. Добрый вечер, Серёжа. Как Лена?

— Зоя! Рад тебя слышать. У нас всё в порядке, спасибо.

— Слушай, Серёжа. Вы _____ в Ярославле в воскресенье?

— Нет. Мы ещё _____ на даче. А почему ты спрашиваешь?

— У меня в воскресенье днём _____ мой внук Денис. Я _____ дома и хочу пригласить (invite) вас на обед.

— Как жаль! Мы не можем в это воскресенье. Может быть в понедельник? Ты _____ свободна в понедельник?

— Жаль, что вы не можете в воскресенье. Конечно, я _____ дома и в понедельник. К сожалению, Денис уже _____ в Москве.

— Понятно.

б. Summarize the main point of Zoya Stepanovna's phone call in a single English sentence.

_____

_____ .

Между нами: Домашние задания   Урок 5: часть 2   **207**

Имя и фамилия: _____   Число: _____

5.6 Упражнéние Е. Трáнспорт

Everyone in our story is on the way somewhere. Use the elements between the slashes to create sentences that tell how our characters are getting to the places mentioned.

1. Зóя Степáновна / éхать / в / большóй / супермáркет / на / автóбус / .

   _____

2. Марáт Азáтович / éхать / в / Самáра / на / машúна / .

   _____

3. Рúмма Юрьевна / éхать / в / Москвá / на / пóезд / .

   _____

4. Нáстя и Макс / éхать / в / парк / на / велосипéд / .

   _____

5. Натáлья Михáйловна / éхать / дом / на / таксú / .

   _____

6. Амáнда / éхать / в / библиотéка / на / метрó / .

   _____

5.6 Упражнéние Ж. Мáленькие словá

Review the conversations in episodes 5.5 and 5.6, and then match each Russian word with its English equivalent.

____ 1. Билéт   а. tomorrow
____ 2. врéмя   б. (it's) expensive
____ 3. Дёшево   в. opens, is opening
____ 4. дóлго   г. I'm in a rush.
____ 5. Дóрого   д. ticket
____ 6. зáвтра   е. (it's) late
____ 7. Здóрово   ж. a long time
____ 8. кудá   з. (to) here
____ 9. Открывáется   и. (it's) cheap
____ 10. Пóздно   к. (to) where
____ 11. Спешý   л. time
____ 12. сюдá   м. cool

Имя и фамилия: _____ Число: _____

5.6 Упражне́ние 3. Ситуа́ции

Review all of the episodes in Часть 2 and indicate what you would say in the following situations.

1. How would you ask a person on the street what time it is?
   _____

2. How would you ask a fellow student at what time the excursion starts?
   _____

3. You and a fellow student have just come out of the library. How would you ask her where she is heading?
   _____

4. How would you ask a fellow student if he wants to study together tomorrow afternoon?
   _____

5. How would you ask a fellow student if she will be free tomorrow at two o'clock?
   _____

Между нами: Дома́шние зада́ния

Уро́к 5: часть 3

5.7 Упражне́ние А. Опя́ть танцу́ют!

The morning after the events of this episode, Caitlin's teacher Mila asks her why she is tired. Below is Caitlin's explanation. Fill in the blanks to describe what happened the previous evening. There are two extra words in the word bank. You do not need to change the forms of any words.

Спят	но́чью	слы́шали
Изве́стные	вре́мя	танцева́ли
Хотя́т	е́здят	пра́вы
Гото́вы	до́ма	ходи́ли
Танцу́ют	забыва́ют	города́х

Ми́ла, э́то це́лая исто́рия. Вчера́ я узна́ла (found out), что сосе́ди Ри́ммы Ю́рьевны и Мара́та Аза́товича — _____ музыка́нты. Они́ вчера́ бы́ли ___ _____, и _____ они́ гро́мко игра́ли на ра́зных инструме́нтах и _____.

Мара́т Аза́тович говори́т, что они́ всё вре́мя игра́ют и _____, не то́лько но́чью, когда́ норма́льные лю́ди _____.

Но э́то непра́вда. Э́ти сосе́ди тепе́рь ре́дко быва́ют (are rarely) до́ма, потому́ что они́ мно́го _____ и выступа́ют (perform). У них конце́рты не то́лько в больши́х _____ Росси́и, но и в Евро́пе. Ра́ньше мои́ хозя́ева ча́сто _____ на их конце́рты, а тепе́рь нет. Ми́ла, мо́жет быть, вы __ _____ о них?

Хотя́ сосе́ди — прекра́сные музыка́нты, Ри́мма Ю́рьевна и Мара́т Аза́тович _____. Э́то пробле́ма, когда́ сосе́ди начина́ют игра́ть но́чью и __ _____, что в э́то вре́мя други́е лю́ди _____ __ спать.

Между нами: Дома́шние зада́ния

5.7 Упражнéние Б. Talking About People

Find all of the adjectives and noun phrases that are used to describe the neighbors in this episode. Some of the phrases are positive or neutral, while others cast the neighbors in a negative light. Write the phrases from the text in the appropriate column.

Сосéди Рѝммы Ю́рьевны и Марáта Азáтовича	
Positive/Neutral	**Negative**

Which three phrases does Marat Azatovich use to describe himself and people like him?

_____   _____   _____

From all of these descriptive terms, one that describes me is: _____.

5.7 Упражне́ние B. How Often?

Sandra, a friend of Caitlin's from Ohio, has just started studying Russian. She wants to send a note to Caitlin about her schedule, but has not yet learned the frequency expressions. Help Sandra complete her sentences by filling in the blanks below.

                                                                                     Я то́же

1. Я _____ встаю́ в семь часо́в. ____
      [usually]

2. Я _____ принима́ю душ. ____
      [every morning]

3. Я _____ за́втракаю до́ма. ____
      [rarely]

4. Я _____ пью ко́фе в кафе́. ____
      [sometimes]

5. Я _____ _____ опа́здываю на заня́тия. ____
      [never]

6. У меня́ ру́сский язы́к _____ ___ _____ _ в де́сять часо́в. ____
                                       [every day]

7. Я _____ _____ смотрю́ телеви́зор. ____
                  [every evening]

8. Я _____ _____ пишу́ эсэмэ́ски. ____
      [all the time]

9. _____ _____ я у́жинаю до́ма у ма́мы. ____
      [every Saturday]

10. _____ _____ я занима́юсь в библиоте́ке. ____
      [every Sunday]

Review the list of Sandra's activities and compare them to your own. If your schedule matches Sandra's, place a check mark in the "**Я то́же**" column on the right.

5.7 Упражнéние Г. Negation

Supply the missing negative phrases based on the English cues. Remember that the **ни-** intensifier in words like **ничегó** can be expressed in English as "nothing" or "anything." Do not forget the **не** before the verb.

1. Зóя Степáновна _____ ____ рабóтает. Онá на пéнсии.
   [not anywhere]

2. Денúс _____ ____ смóтрит телевúзор. Врéмени нет!
   [never]

3. Сегóдня Амáнда отдыхáет. Онá _____ ____ дéлает!
   [not anything]

4. Джош сегóдня _____ ____ идёт. Он óчень устáл пóсле концéрта.
   [(to) nowhere]

5. В сентябрé Тóни _____ ____ знал в Россúи, а тепéрь он знáет Олéга.
   [no one]

6. Сейчáс конéц семéстра. Все устáли, и _____ ____ хóчет занимáться.
   [no one]

5.7 Упражнéние Д. Хóбби

Caitlin is talking about her and her friends' interests. Fill in the blanks with appropriate forms of the verb **ходúть** to complete her description.

— Вы ужé знáете, что я люблю́ мýзыку, и поэ́тому чáсто _____ на концéрты. Здесь в Казáни моя́ подрýга Сáра лю́бит джаз, и иногдá мы вмéсте _____ в клуб. Амáнда лю́бит искýсство и чáсто _____ в Рýсский музéй. Тóни тепéрь знáет Ю́рия Николáевича, дя́дю Денúса, котóрый рабóтает в теáтре. Онú вмéсте _____ на спектáкли.

— Мúла, кудá вы _____, éсли не секрéт?

5.7 Упражнéние Е. Бúзнес

Marat Azatovich is discussing all of the traveling that he does for work. Fill in the blanks with appropriate present-tense forms of the verb **éздить** to complete his description.

Жизнь бизнесмéна в Россúи óчень трýдная. Я чáсто _____ в рáзные городá. Мой партнёр в бúзнесе тóже мнóго _____. Иногдá мы вмéсте _____, éсли э́то серьёзный клиéнт. Женá чáсто спрáшивает меня́: «Марáт, почемý ты так чáсто _____ в небольшúе городá?» Я отвечáю, что бизнесмéны _____ тудá, где нахóдятся клиéнты.

5.7 Упражнéние Ж. Нáши тéмы

a. The sentences below suggest topics that you and your friends might discuss. Fill in the blanks with frequency adverbs (e.g., **никогдá не**, **рéдко**, **иногдá**, **чáсто**, **всё врéмя**) to make each sentence true for you and your friends.

1. Мы _____ разговáриваем о нóвых фи́льмах.
2. Мы _____ разговáриваем об интерéсных сáйтах в интернéте.
3. Мы _____ разговáриваем о нáших преподавáтелях.
4. Мы _____ разговáриваем о нáших заня́тиях в университéте.
5. Мы _____ разговáриваем о нáших сосéдях.
6. Мы _____ разговáриваем о нáших роди́телях.
7. Мы _____ разговáриваем об актёрах в Голливýде.
8. Мы _____ разговáриваем об извéстных музыкáнтах

б. Review the sentences above and circle the nouns that are in the prepositional plural.

5.8 Упражнéние А. Свобóдное врéмя

Match the beginning of each sentence with a conclusion that reflects comments made in this episode.

____ 1. Расскажи́те, пожáлуйста, что вы   а. в интернéте.
____ 2. Кéйтлин фотографи́рует   б. неинтерéсная жизнь.
____ 3. Дóма Мáрша кáждый день   в. свобóдного врéмени.
____ 4. Другие студéнты всё врéмя   г. цéркви, мечéти, пáмятники.
____ 5. Си́нди говори́т, что у них нет   д. дéлаете в свобóдное врéмя.
____ 6. Хозя́ева Бóбби éздят на   е. éздит на прирóду.
____ 7. Кéйтлин говори́т, какáя у Си́нди   ж. дáчу, где рабóтают в садý.
____ 8. Когдá погóда хорóшая, Ми́ла   з. бéгает.

5.8 Упражнéние Б. Свобóдное врéмя

Match each Russian phrase to its English equivalent. Practice saying the Russian phrases aloud as you work.

____ 1.	ходи́ть по го́роду	а.	to go to the gym
____ 2.	фотографи́ровать	б.	to watch TV
____ 3.	бе́гать	в.	to walk around town
____ 4.	пла́вать	г.	to go on excursions
____ 5.	ходи́ть в фи́тнес-це́нтр	д.	to watch a TV series
____ 6.	ходи́ть в музе́й	е.	to go to the movies
____ 7.	ходи́ть в кино́	ж.	to work in the garden
____ 8.	ходи́ть на экску́рсии	з.	to take pictures
____ 9.	смотре́ть телеви́зор	и.	to take a walk in the forest
____ 10.	рабо́тать в саду́	к.	to run, jog
____ 11.	ходи́ть по магази́нам	л.	to go to a museum
____ 12.	игра́ть в ка́рты	м.	to go on a trip to the countryside
____ 13.	смотре́ть сериа́лы	н.	to swim
____ 14.	е́здить на приро́ду	о.	to go around to stores (to shop)
____ 15.	гуля́ть в лесу́	п.	to play cards

5.8 Упражнéние В. Какóе спряжéние? (Which Conjugation?)

Sort the Russian phrases in 5.8 Упражне́ние Б according to their conjugation patterns. Write the whole verb phrase in the appropriate column.

1st conjugation with stems in -ай- / -яй- (e.g., чита́ть)	-ова-ть verbs	2nd conjugation with no mutation (e.g., по́мнить)	2nd conjugation with д > ж mutation

5.8 Упражнéние Г. Что вы дéлаете в свобóдное врéмя?

Using the verb phrases in 5.8 Упражнéние Б, or other verb phrases that you might have encountered, write ten sentences answering the question, "**Что вы дéлаете в свобóдное врéмя?**" You can use frequency adverbs (e.g., **никогдá не**, **рéдко**, **иногдá**, **чáсто**, **всё врéмя**, **кáждую недéлю**, etc.) to give more nuance to your answers. Write out the phrase "**В свобóдное врéмя**" at the start of at least three of your sentences. One has been done for you as an example.

0. В свобóдное врéмя я рéдко хожý по магазúнам.

1. ___
2. ___
3. ___
4. ___
5. ___
6. ___
7. ___
8. ___
9. ___
10. ___

🎧 5.8 Упражне́ние Д. Round-Trip or Heading to

a. Listen to the recording and fill in the missing blank for each sentence.

	makes round trips	headed to; on one's way	going by vehicle
1. Я _____ в библиоте́ку.	____	____	____
2. Мы _____ в кино́.	____	____	____
3. Мы _____ на да́чу.	____	____	____
4. Мара́т Аза́тович _____ на рабо́ту.	____	____	____
5. Моя́ хозя́йка _____ в це́рковь.	____	____	____
6. На́ши сосе́ди _____ в Чика́го на рок-конце́рт.	____	____	____
7. Куда́ вы _____?	____	____	____
8. Куда́ вы _____?	____	____	____
9. Куда́ ты _____?	____	____	____
10. Куда́ ты _____?	____	____	____
11. Я _____ домо́й.	____	____	____
12. Студе́нты _____ на заня́тия.	____	____	____

б. Re-read the sentences above and place a check mark in the appropriate column to indicate whether the people make regular round trips to a destination or whether they are heading to a destination. Place a check mark in the last column if the verb makes it clear that the person is using a vehicle to get to that destination.

5.9 Упражнéние А. Что они́ сего́дня де́лали?

a. When talking about what a person has done during the day, you can say either:
   - where a person has been (**быть** + **в/на** + prepositional case) OR
   - to where a person has made a trip (**ходи́ть/е́здить** + **в/на** + accusative)

In the sentences below, select the verb that makes each sentence grammatically correct.

	Ве́рно и́ли неве́рно
1. Ке́йтлин [**была́** / **ходи́ла**] на рабо́ту.	____
2. Джош [**был** / **ходи́л**] на хоро́шем конце́рте.	____
3. Ама́нда [**была́** / **е́здила**] в Чебокса́ры.	____
4. То́ни [**был** / **ходи́л**] на экску́рсию.	____
5. Ри́мма Ю́рьевна [**была́** / **ходи́ла**] на рабо́те.	____
6. Мара́т Аза́тович [**был** / **е́здил**] в командиро́вке.	____
7. Зо́я Степа́новна [**была́** / **ходи́ла**] до́ма.	____
8. Светла́на Бори́совна [**была́** / **е́здила**] на вы́ставку.	____

б. Write in **В** (for **Ве́рно**) in the right-hand column above if the content of the sentence matches the events in the text or **Н** (for **Неве́рно**) if it does not match the events in the text.

5.9 Упражне́ние Б. Ситуа́ции

Review all of the episodes in Часть 3 and indicate what you would say in the following situations.

1. How would you ask a roommate if she hears music?

2. How would your roommate tell you that it is the neighbors, and that they play [their] instruments every evening?

3. How would you explain that your neighbors often go to Moscow and St. Petersburg?

4. How would you tell someone that talking loudly is not allowed here?

5. How would you ask a group of students what they do in their free time?

6. How would you ask a fellow student if he jogs or swims?

7. How would you complain that you have no free time?

Между ними: Дома́шние зада́ния

🔎 5.9 Упражнение В. Фа́кты. Собы́тия. Лю́ди.

On mezhdunami.dropmark.com you will find links that advertise various public events. Open any four of the links and examine the advertisement closely. Try to sound out unfamiliar words. Notice that the day precedes the month [01.04 = April 1st].

Fill in as much information as you can about the event in the table below. You can write in English or Russian.

# of link	What is the event?	Date?	Time?	Location?

5.9 Упражне́ние Г. Сочине́ние

You work with an international student exchange group, and a student from Russia will be visiting your campus soon. The student has written you an email asking about a typical weekday for you, and what you do on weekends. Write a response that includes information on your class schedule as well as what you do in your free time.

Caitlin's email letter in episode 5.3 is an excellent model for your response. Organize your answer into logical sections describing your morning routine, your classes, and your evening activities. Be sure to include time expressions and adverbs of frequency.

Your response should be at least 75-words long and should include a greeting and a closing. Stay within the bounds of the Russian that you know.

Image Information

5.1 Упражнéние В. В какóй день?
"Blank Stick Note Clip Art is in the public domain. Last accessed October 28, 2015.
http://www.clker.com/clipart-blank-sticky-note-2.html

5.4 Упражнéние А. Скóлько сейчáс врéмени?
"Analogue clock face.svg" by Tkgd2007 is licensed under CC by 3.0. Last accessed October 28, 2015.
https://commons.wikimedia.org/wiki/File:Analogue_clock_face.svg

5.5 Упражнéние В. Билéты (Tickets)?
Map created by Di Shi, Director of Cartographic Services Lab, University of Kansas. Released under a CC BY license.